JESUS
WHO IS HE?

HOW TO FIND MEANING AND HEALING IN YOUR LIFE
THROUGH THE LIFE OF JESUS CHRIST

JOHN AND MILLIE YOUNGBERG
Fellow travelers on the upward way

Illustrated by NATHAN GREENE
Making the way more beautiful and the signposts clearer

Cover illustration: Stephen Gjertson, *Peace, Be Still*
Design and layout: Glesni Mason
Illustration coordination: Bonnie Greene
Editors: Tim Lale and Candice Hollingsead

Illustrations by Nathan Greene, © 1988-2015, All Rights Reserved, Used By Permission. www.nathangreene.com

2 4 6 8 9 7 5 3 1
ISBN: 978-0-692-45337-7

TABLE OF CONTENTS

INTRODUCTION

We find disorientation around us today in every facet and realm of society. Perhaps in your life there is upheaval and brokenness. We belong to the human race, part of the seven-billion-plus who live on planet Earth, with all the trouble that goes with it. There may be ideas or other things that separate us, but we venture the thought that we have much more in common than we have differences between us. We are all in this together.

Every one of us is searching for meaning. We long to make relationships. Our life is a quest to find these. Some search on one path, and some on another. The purpose of this little book is to examine the question: Can we find meaning in Jesus? Does His life offer meaning to us in our quest? WHO IS HE?

Our purpose is not apologetics, not to argue with those who believe differently. Whether you count yourself as belonging to Generation X, Generation Z, whether you are a Millennial or a Baby-boomer sojourning on life's pathway, whether you go to church or don't go, whether you're Christian, Muslim, Jewish, Hindu, Buddhist, atheist, agnostic, or whatever—welcome! We are going on our quest to find meaning.

Among the people who have thought it through, there is little doubt that a historical man named Jesus lived in the first century AD. Writers in the first and early second centuries refer to Him often. These include the Roman writer Tacitus, the Roman governor Pliny the Younger, and the Jewish historian Josephus. Thousands of Jesus believers in those centuries chose to refuse emperor worship even though it meant death, chose to maintain their allegiance to Jesus at the cost of their lives. This is strong evidence that thousands and perhaps hundreds of thousands had no question in their minds that Jesus had lived on earth and was the correct object of their worship. So we begin with the assumption that the stories about His life are real and true.

However, that does not necessarily mean this Jesus has claims on you and me today. So, in these pages we will go beyond the historical and doctrinal evidence and ask, Does the Jesus presented in the Bible meet the needs of people today? Can we find meaning and healing in our relationship with Him? Join us on that quest for answers.

This book is all about Jesus, who Jesus is, and beyond that it is about you and all you can be as a person. It's about your relationship with others, your family, your health, and becoming a New You that will amaze yourself and others. It's also about personal healing and breaking the chains that bind us to the past and giving us freedom to go forward as a new person. It's about helping you in your choices and choice making to choose a new path that will give you peace and lead to a new lifestyle and success in the things which you attempt.

How to use this book. Take time daily to read portions of this book, personally or with family, or invite neighbors and friends in a home group setting for an hour once a week to expand your knowledge. At the end of each chapter there are reflection items that will enhance the chapter's message as you discuss the questions with each other. Enjoy!

NOTE

Although this book is based on historical research and archaeological data, in order to make it thought-provoking to the contemporary mind, the authors have taken the liberty to put words into the mouths of various characters that reflect their situation, sometimes with a modern twist. Learn together and have a blessed experience—Just grow!

PEACE AFTER THE STORM

t had been what you might call "the busy day." Among the many happenings, Jesus healed a blind and dumb man. Jesus' brothers and mother came to a house where He was speaking and tried to take Him back home to Nazareth, because they thought He was embarrassing the family. He went down to the beach and shared the "Sermon by the Sea," sitting in a boat so the crowd could see and hear Him. There He uttered nine parables to a huge multitude. Then He said to the disciples, "Let's cross to the other side of the lake."

Evening has fallen. Tired with the ceaseless activity of "the busy day," Jesus is physically and emotionally spent. He lies down on a pillow in the back of the boat, and within moments He is sound asleep. The evening is calm, clear, and pleasant.

Without warning, a violent wind storm comes up. The waves, whipped into a fury by the howling winds, dash fiercely over the boat and threaten to engulf it. It sounds like a symphony of demons as the wind roars around the twelve disciples. They sense that their lives are in great danger.

Faces are furrowed with fear as the disciples battle against the gale. Their muscles bulge as they strain at the oars. They struggle with all their might, some rowing and some bailing water—but it is no use. In spite of their desperate attempts to save their own lives in this ferocious storm, the waves are breaking right into the boat.

STORM ON THE LAKE

This kind of wind storm is not unusual on the Sea of Galilee. The lake is about 696 feet (212 meters) below sea level. Just a few miles north is Mount Hermon, the highest mountain in the region, with an elevation of 9,232 feet (2,814 meters). When the warm air on the lake rises, it is often replaced by cold air blowing off Mount Hermon, or down the ravines from the Gilead Plateau, whipping the lake into a violent tempest.

Suddenly a streak of lightning pierces the darkness, and the disciples remember what they have forgotten. There is Jesus, peacefully sleeping in the stern of the boat. Now they realize that He is their only hope.

"Jesus," they shout above the shrieking wind, "don't You care that we are all about to drown?"

Jesus awakes. He stands up in the heaving boat, no fear on His face. With faith in His Father above that the lives of the 13 will be spared until their mission is complete, He raises His hand and speaks to the wind and the waves.

"Peace! Be still!"

And suddenly there's a great, eerie calm. The lake becomes as smooth as glass!

Jesus *rebukes* the waves. "Why were you afraid? Where is your faith?" Jesus asks.

The disciples are filled with awe and amazement. They marvel at what just happened. It was a miraculous moment that snatched them from what seemed like a watery grave to complete calm.

The water-soaked men say to one another, "Who is this man? WHO IS HE? that even the winds and waves obey him?"

That question echoes in the portals of our hearts. Who Is He that is there when we need Him the most? Can Jesus control the storms of my life and give me peace?

REFLECTION

1. As you recall the details of the story, what is it saying to you?
2. Have you ever felt as though you were rowing like mad to save your job, your marriage, your family, your sanity, and it felt as though you were all alone? And somehow you made it through. Who is it that has made this possible? How?
3. The golden sun may cast its brilliant, warm rays on your finances, relationships, health, and suddenly howling winds unleash their fury against the ship of your life. You too, like the disciples, are fighting for survival. The funnel cloud of darkness and dread is spiraling you down in the stormy sea of destruction and death. Like the disciples, have you cried out, "Master, Lord, Savior, Friend—save me! I perish!"? Share your story.
4. Have you seen Jesus helping others in the storms of life? Discuss.

JESUS–WHO IS HE?

He is the Giver of Peace—the One Who Calms the Storms. When Jesus spoke to the wind and the waves and there was a great calm, the amazed disciples said to each other, "Who is this man? WHO IS HE?" This book seeks for an answer to this question.

The Bible calls Jesus "the Prince of Peace" (Isaiah 9:6). At Jesus' birth, according to the Bible, the angel choir sang "Glory to God in the highest and on earth PEACE, good will toward men." Does He really bring peace?

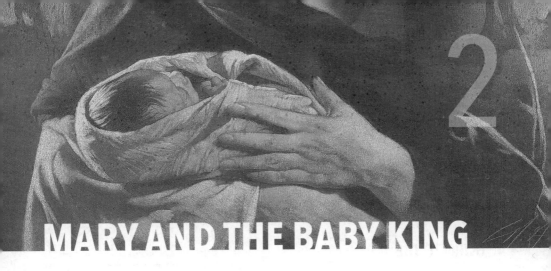

MARY AND THE BABY KING

I f you have children or grandchildren, you can never forget when the first one was born. When our daughter-in-law had gone to the maternity unit expecting our first grandchild, relatives descended from three states. One drove twelve hours to be there. Four grandparents, parents, and two siblings gathered for the great family event. Finally one grandmother came running down the hall to the waiting room, all smiles, shouting, "It's a girl! It's a girl!" Minutes later we were in the obstetrical care unit as the precious bundle, whose big blue eyes focused on ours, was lovingly passed from person to person.

This was the evening of Good Friday, and the sun was about to go down. Truly the day had double significance as a new life came into the world. The labor was over.

What did the inn keeper think of the very pregnant Mary when he said, "Sorry, every room is taken and every bed is full? But if you like, you can sleep in the stable." He wasn't tuned in to whispers from on high that were trying to tell him that the long awaited King would be born of Mary that very night. The sheep and the donkey looked on. Did they understand more than the inn keeper? The shepherds were talking about the coming Savior on that chilly starry night out in the hills near Bethlehem. They were waiting for the Advent, listening, trying to hear God's voice. To them the angel appeared proclaiming in their ears the most stupendous news of all history. "Peace on earth. Good will to men." Jesus was born in Bethlehem. Can you see them rushing to the stable and peering into the manger, recognizing the Baby King? The Wise Men listened as God led them to search the Old Testament Scriptures. While others turned blinded eyes, they followed the star. They gave their finest gifts—gold, frankincense and myrrh—to the amazed couple. This supported Joseph, Mary, and the Infant Jesus, as they fled to Egypt avoiding the murderous plot of Herod the Great.

BORN TO DIE

We rejoice when babies are born—they are born to live. But this Baby was different. He was born to die! Forty days after his birth, Mary and Joseph lovingly brought Baby Jesus to the temple to have Him dedicated and His name inscribed in the temple records.

"Simeon, where are you going?" a friend asked. He says "Hi!" but he does not linger. He's on a mission. Nothing will distract him. He has been waiting for this day for many years. God had revealed to him that he would see the Savior of the world before he died. He is very old now, but he comes to the temple, led by the Holy Spirit, at the precise moment that Jesus, the promised Messiah, is being dedicated. He received the precious bundle in his arms. As he spoke, an astonished Mary and Joseph caught his words. "This child is meant for the rising and falling of many. I've waited a lifetime to see the coming of the Messiah. Now, Lord, let Your servant depart in peace." Then, as the Holy Spirit inspired Simeon's words to Mary, he added, "A sword shall pierce through your own soul, that the thoughts of many hearts may be revealed."

Mary receives an inkling of what is coming. Like the sunset that begins to cast shadows across the earth, announcing the approaching night, so she is given a glimpse of what Jesus' mission will cost in order to save fallen, broken humanity, enveloped in darkness. One day the sun would set completely, and His life would be snuffed out in the blackness of night. But even in the darkness of night, His death would be a sign of His love and mercy to those who accept Him and choose Him as Lord and Savior.

THE RIGHT GENES?

Can I excuse my actions by saying, "I've got bad genes. I got that trait from my grandmother, and my Uncle Joe had the same problem." It's true that we receive genetic tendencies from our ancestors. But that doesn't mean we are predetermined. We have 20,000 genes which we can't change, but around those genes are epigenes which are like light switches which turn a given gene ON or OFF. We also receive from our parents given settings of the epigenes, but it is within the power of our frontal lobe of the brain, by God's help, to change those settings.

We don't know a lot about the ancestral genes that Jesus received through Mary's line. Did Mary elect to nourish certain character tendencies from her ancestors and deliberately reject other tendencies? Apparently so because her ancestors included David, Bathsheba and Rahab (Matthew 1:6,7; Luke 1:32). Mary of Nazareth left behind unwanted genetic expressions and by her choices, healthy lifestyle, and walk with God became a living example of becoming what God wanted her to be. We too can be victorious over hereditary and cultivated tendencies toward evil. Transformational change is possible and you can do it!

AN UNUSUAL LOVE STORY

She was young, vibrant, and compassionate. Like life in spring, like a blossoming flower, Mary was spiritual and had a special divine relationship that qualified her for being the mother of Jesus. She had the character and abilities needed for raising God's Son for the mission of His life. Mary had memorized many of the sacred writings of her people and had heard the historical stories passed from one generation to another. Many years before, one of her ancestors had been a most famous king. Despite being of the royal line, she was poor.

Where Mary lived, there resided another descendant of the royal line. His name was Joseph. He was a carpenter in the little town of several hundred inhabitants. Tragedy had struck his home. His wife died, leaving him with at least six children to care for, perhaps more (Mark 6:3).

He had noticed her, and young Mary returned Joseph's fond glances. Perhaps it was one day when Mary's parents were at the carpenter shop ordering a piece of furniture that he asked if he might marry their daughter. She was a beautiful, yet unassuming young lady. The marriage was arranged for sometime in the future.

MARY OF NAZARETH–WHO WAS SHE?

Mary was of the lineage of King David. This woman was to bring greater blessing to the world than any other woman in history. When the angel appeared to her with the astounding announcement that she would be the mother of the long-awaited Messiah, the Savior of the world, she was willing. She "believed" (Luke 1:45), even though the angel Gabriel's word was contrary to natural law. Young Mary said, "Behold the maidservant of the Lord! Let it be to me according to your word" (Luke 1:38).

What a contrast with others who doubted. Zachariah doubted the same angel's prophecy that he and his wife Elizabeth would become parents of John the Baptist even in their advanced years. Also, the national leaders in Jerusalem doubted and refused to go to Bethlehem to look for the newborn king, although they met the wise men who came from the East in search of Him, and in spite of the fact they undoubtedly heard reports about the angels who had appeared to the shepherds. Perhaps the leaders resented the fact that they had been passed by and the message had gone to poor shepherds and foreign magi. Some might not believe, "but Mary kept all these things and pondered them in her heart" (Luke 2:19).

The angel Gabriel said to her, "Rejoice, highly favored one." Mary was highly favored by heaven; God's smile was on her because she would submit to the plan the angel Gabriel announced to her, even if it would compromise her reputation by making her an unwed mother. While human beings tend to "favor" someone because they have high standing, natural talents, or beauty, heaven "favored" Mary although she was of "lowly state" (Luke 1:48, 52, 53) because of her spirit. Her soul magnified the Lord, and her spirit rejoiced in God her Savior (Luke 1:47).

Mary embodied the core values of a good mother but also the core values of heaven. Her love was caring, patient, gentle, and graceful. She nursed at her breast the One who had created the worlds and the human family. She taught Him to walk, to develop His speech. She sang to Him from the Psalms, taught Him to pray and read, taught Him lessons from nature. Not only did she reflect the love of God, but the love of God flowed through her, and in that outpouring of love for Jesus, the Father God Himself was loving His own Son fleshed in Mary. Mary's life serves as an example to all mothers today as they bring up their children in the care and nurture of the Lord.

WHO IS THIS CHILD?

The angel gave the name of Jesus to both Mary and Joseph. The prophet Isaiah, 750 years earlier, called His name Immanuel, which means "God With Us." Jesus means Savior. Yes, here was the Savior of the world, God With Us, in the form of a baby!

The birth of Jesus was marked by poverty. Royal palaces would have been honored to have the King of the Universe grace their marbled rooms with His presence, but Jesus was born in a stable. He was cradled not in gold and gem-studded furniture but in a manger—an eating place for animals!

THE DEDICATION

Let's follow this special couple and the infant Jesus when He was brought to the temple to be dedicated. The priest on duty asked the name of the child. "Jesus" was Mary and Joseph's response. The name was duly written in the temple records. The priest saw nothing special in the occasion. Joseph and Mary were poor, as he noted from the sacrifice of two pigeons they brought. (People who were well off would offer a lamb, but the law permitted poorer people to offer a pair of turtledoves or two young pigeons.) Then the priest took the infant in his arms and dedicated Him to the Lord. It was only a ritual to him. Maybe on his day of duty he would dedicate many children and this was just one more. Would no one recognize the Savior of the world?

At that moment, Simeon enters the scene. "This man was just and devout, waiting for the Consolation of Israel, and the Holy Spirit was upon him" (Luke 2:25). The Holy Spirit had revealed to him that he would see the Savior of the world before he died. Seeing Jesus as a baby was the most sacred and memorable moment of his life.

TEACHING JESUS IN CHILDHOOD

With the Hebrew Scriptures, Mary taught the dawning intelligence of the Child Jesus the very words He had spoken to God's people centuries before in Old Testament times. Mary may have obtained access to the scrolls from the local synagogue. Probably in her childhood she had memorized large portions of the Hebrew Bible. Now at His mother's knee the Child Jesus learned the very words He had spoken to God's people centuries before in Old Testament times.

In her study Mary was made aware of Scripture truth previously given to Isaiah. She was a spiritual person living by every word that God had revealed. This may be one reason the Father called her to be the mother of Jesus—the Savior of the world.

When Simeon dedicated Jesus, the child's mother reflected on what Isaiah had written. How her heart must have thrilled as she recalled portions of the prophet Isaiah she had memorized.

"Behold, the virgin shall conceive and bear a Son, and shall call His name Immanuel" (Isaiah 7:14). "For a child has been born—for us! the gift of a son—for us! He'll take over the running of the world. His names will be: Amazing Counselor,

Strong God, Eternal Father, Prince of Wholeness.
His ruling authority will grow,
and there'll be no limits to the wholeness he brings"
(Isaiah 9:6, 7, MSG).

Under Mary's care, "the child grew, and waxed strong in spirit, filled with wisdom: and the grace of God was upon Him" (Luke 2:40, KJV). From childhood He was possessed of one purpose: to bless others.

COMING OF AGE

It was the Jewish custom that when a male child reached the age of twelve, considered the age of accountability, he was to accompany his parents to the Jewish feasts. Luke records this visit of the boy Jesus to the temple in Jerusalem. The Child who had been memorizing and living Old Testament Scripture during His formative years came to the temple. Can you see Him there? Perhaps He is witnessing the slaying of the lamb and He begins to understand that He is the Lamb being foreshadowed. Perhaps Jesus begins to understand that someday He will be sacrificed, and His blood will take away the sin of the world. As this Youth stands there enthralled, God is unveiling His plans to Him.

After Jesus became separated from Mary and Joseph, His parents started home thinking that He was with friends in the traveling group. In the evening they searched diligently and, not finding Him, started back for Jerusalem. They finally found their Son in the temple, listening to and asking questions of the instructors of the law and the scholars of the nation, demonstrating His amazing knowledge and application of Scripture. Never before had these scholars seen such wisdom in any of their hundreds and perhaps thousands of scholars! When Mary said, "Son, we have searched for You three days! Why have You treated us like this?" Jesus' answer was the keynote of His later ministry: "Why did you seek Me? Did you not know that I must be about My Father's business?" The Gospel writer Luke's account of Jesus' adolescence ends with the sublime statement of His development: "And Jesus increased in wisdom [mentally] and stature [physically] and in favor with God [spiritually] and man [socially]" (Luke 2:52).

The Scripture records no events in the life of Jesus between the age of twelve and thirty. Some call these the "silent years" or the "hidden years." During those years, Joseph passed away and Jesus toiled at the carpenter's trade. Without any doubt He was sympathetic and compassionate, lightened people's heavy burdens, and encouraged them on the upward path. He hid the treasured Bible verses in His heart, and "It is written" was often on His lips. He performed no miracles then, but as the adolescents and young adults of today often do, He reached out His willing hands and blessed others.

THE KING BORN TO DIE

Our eyes have scanned so many other objects that brought no light, no meaning, no happiness, no hope, no peace. In the moment we behold the Savior, we no longer see our shame, guilt, anger, sadness, hate. But we see His love, mercy, grace, forgiveness, peace, and joy. Yes, when we lock eyes with Jesus, we too are born to die—die to our pride, die to our shame, die to our hurts, die to our failures, die to rejection.

The Baby King, born to die, is a story of contrasts:
- He who came to give life and give it more abundantly is given death by the people He came to save.
- He was the Light rejected by the people in darkness (John 1:4, 5).
- He came to His own, and His own did not receive Him (John 1:11).
- He who created all things is scorned by His own creation.

Our lives may also turn out to be living contrasts.
- We marry desiring long life and happiness but find ourselves in a divorce courtroom.
- We desire health but find ourselves suffering from cancer.

- We try to live at peace, yet we find ourselves victims of abuse.

But like our example Jesus, we find that after the trial comes the triumph and the victory.

Can a mother today nurture and educate her child to grow in favor with God and man?

Dr. Aric Sigman writing in The British Medical Association's *Archives of Disease in Childhood* states that "Screen time appears to have created the three-parent family"—Mother, Father and the TV.

By the age of seven, a child born today will have spent a full year glued to screens. Can our children blossom and live in favor with God and man on this kind of routine? Do our children find time to memorize Scripture, pray, enjoy nature and help others?

REFLECTION

1. What do the life of Mary and the early life of Jesus say to you?
2. How can we be "favored," even "highly favored," by God as Mary was?
3. Recall the young Jesus' story. How do you prepare to be used by God? Who is Jesus for you?
4. Can the heavenly messenger, our guardian angel, say of us, "The Lord is with you; blessed are you among women/men"? Reflect on this.

JESUS–WHO IS HE?

He is the Promised Child, Immanuel—"God With Us"—the long-awaited Messiah, Jesus of Nazareth, the Baby who was born to die.

3
SPECIAL MOMENTS TO REMEMBER FOREVER

The angel told Mary that her relative Elizabeth was in the sixth month of her pregnancy, so Mary rushed down from Nazareth to the little village near the wilderness of Judea where Elizabeth lived. As Mary came through the doorway of the house and greeted her with a smile, the babe in Elizabeth's womb leaped for joy (Luke 1:41). It was as though the baby knew it was in the presence of Someone special. Mary was also pregnant, so the two women had something in common to share as they visited. The unborn little one who, at birth three months later, would be named John, reflected Elizabeth's joy. Caught up in this special moment, Mary burst into what today is called the Song of Mary and said: "My soul magnifies the Lord, and my spirit has rejoiced in God my Savior" (Luke 1:47). "God my Savior" was Jesus in Mary's womb. The aged Elizabeth would probably not live to see the beginning of their children's ministries thirty years later, but she would always remember this special moment when her unborn babe leaped for joy.

The pregnant mother's state of mind—happiness or sadness—profoundly affects the unborn child. Researchers believe that the intrauterine environment is even more important in the physiologic and emotional influence of the child than are the genetic factors.

Peter Nathanielsz, M.D., PhD writes: "there is mounting evidence that programming of lifetime health by the conditions in the womb is equally, if not more important, than our genes in determining how we perform mentally and physically during life." Negativity or a positive attitude during pregnancy can alter neural development and affect genetic expression, according to new research in the field of epigenetics.

AT THE CARPENTRY SHOP IN NAZARETH

Jesus lived a simple, quiet, and secluded life with His mother Mary and the family in Nazareth until the appointed time to begin His public ministry. Living a sinless life in a blended family with at least six older stepsiblings was not easy. Yet day by day through Jesus' childhood, youth, and young adulthood, the townspeople noted His beautiful, compassionate character, how He met the needs of others, how He brought hope, love, and encouragement to all around Him.

Each morning at dawn and again at eventide, Jesus can be found kneeling out in the nature He had created, and daily the Father unfolds His plans to Jesus. He is aware of His future mission that weighs upon Him. There in the beauty of God's nature, He prays and waits, knowing that God His Father will reveal His plans in His own way and time. Jesus lives in solitude and obscurity until the moment arrives when His mission must be announced to the world.

One day He is working at the carpenter's shop that had been Joseph's. Perhaps Jesus has a saw or a chisel in His hand as He carves on a tongue-and-groove joint to unite the boards for a cradle or a chair. Suddenly the door bursts open and one of the inhabitants of Nazareth rushes in and excitedly says, "I have just arrived back from the Jordan River. A man named John dressed in camel's hair is preaching a startling message. He is calling sinners to repent and to be baptized and wash away their sins. Thousands from all over Judea and even Galilee are flocking to hear Him!" The news of John the Baptist's message has arrived even in remote Nazareth.

Jesus seems transfixed. He is silent for a number of seconds, and then He thoughtfully hangs up the saw, puts the chisel in its place, and sweeps up the wood shavings from the carpenter's bench and the floor. He now knows His work in Joseph's carpentry shop has come to an end.

It's a God-ordained, divine moment that will live forever. Jesus realizes His time has come, and He prepares to make the journey to the Jordan. He says goodbye to Mary and His family and moves toward His destined ministry that was planned before His coming to earth. Now at about the age of thirty, He hears not just the report of a fellow townsman but the divine call. Jesus joins the multitude heading south some sixty or seventy miles to where John is preaching.

THINK ABOUT IT

Even if you have worked as a farmer or day-laborer for many years, could there come a day when God calls you to leave your tractor, your eight-hour shift at the factory, or your government service job and move to another place, to share with others what God has done in your life?

JOHN AND JESUS MEET FACE TO FACE

One day John is preaching and baptizing when he sees Someone on the river bank coming towards him. Although he has never met Jesus before, John recognizes that he is looking on the face of Jesus of Nazareth. He is awed as he senses a holy presence. Again his heart leaps with holy excitement as it did thirty years before, when his mother, Elizabeth, greeted Mary the mother of Jesus. John recognizes in the Man a purity of life and holiness of character he has seen in no other.

As they meet face to face, Jesus gently says, "John, I've come to be baptized." John is astonished by the request of this Holy One.

He remonstrates with Him, saying, "Jesus, You should baptize me." But Jesus insists, not because He needs spiritual cleansing but because He desires to leave an example for all of us who want our sins to be washed away. John the Baptist obeys and leads Him into the current of the river and immerses Him, burying Him in the waters of the Jordan. Jesus comes up out of the water and, with His head dripping, makes His way to the bank, where He kneels and pours out His soul in prayer to His Father, who had chosen Him for such a time as this.

Never has John heard such a prayer. He sees the Majesty of Heaven kneeling and hears Him reaching out to His Father in tears as He starts this journey to the cross of Calvary. He hears Him agonizing with heaven, pleading for power to overcome. Jesus pleads for assurance and for the testimony from above that His Father accepts His ministry in humanity. There is a solemnity of divine presence as the heavens open. It is a sacred moment between heaven and earth.

A white dove descends from above in heavenly radiance and hovers over the head of Jesus. Myriads of angels would have delighted in bearing to earth the answer to Jesus' prayer, but no! The Father Himself speaks, and His voice reverberates in the ears of the thousands gathered that day at the Jordan: "This is My beloved Son, in whom I am well pleased."

Yes, heaven itself has proclaimed in thunderous tones on this, the inauguration day of Jesus' ministry, that He is called by God, that He is the Son of God, that the Father is well pleased with Him. Upon receiving this affirmation, Jesus is ready to go forward.

John must have looked in wonder at what was happening before his eyes. It must have been a majestic, once-in-a-lifetime, supremely awesome moment. Extending his hand toward Jesus, he exclaims, "Behold the Lamb of God who takes away the sin of the world."

Jesus has accepted the call. He is accepted as the Beloved Son. He now begins His public ministry as the Messiah King and Lamb of God, "filled with the Spirit." His mission embraces every son and daughter of Adam and Eve from ancient times and extends down through the ages to all of us who live today.

Have I heard the Father say, "You are My beloved son, My beloved daughter, in whom I am well pleased"?

REFLECTION

1. Describe in your own words to someone the special events that took place at the Jordan River and how these impressed you.
2. What special moments do you remember that changed your life forever? Share with someone.
3. As Jesus began His earthly ministry by praying to His Father God for direction, so can you. Find the right time and right place to have a prayerful talk with your Father God about His plan for you.

JESUS–WHO IS HE?

Ask John the Baptist. "He is the Lamb of God who takes away the sin of the world. I heard the voice of the Father, who said, 'This is My Beloved Son in whom I am well pleased.'" He is the One who heard the divine call and answered it. He is the One who calls you and me.

VICTORY OVER THE TEMPTER

The words, "You are My beloved Son, in whom I am well pleased" were spoken at Jesus' baptism, announcing His public ministry. But what came next? A grand parade with an honor guard? Banners waving and trumpets blaring while the public shouts His praises?

Jesus did not come to earth to receive earthly honor. He gave up the scepter of universal acclaim and heavenly glory. Jesus came instead "to seek and to save that which was lost" (Luke 19:10). If this is true, then He would have to go back to where Adam and Eve lost their way and gain the victory in those same points. He must conquer where they were conquered.

Not too far from Jericho and the Jordan Valley were desolate, rugged mountains. After His baptism, to this wilderness Jesus directed His footsteps so that He could have undistracted time to reflect on His mission and communicate with His Father about His sacred work.

In our own lives, when we're struggling to make plans, we often encounter a slithering, sly intruder who tempts us to make wrong choices—one who says, "This is a better way—follow me." Satan, the usurping ruler of this earth, particularly targets Jesus at the beginning of His work. He appears in the desert and offers Jesus attractive options that would deviate from the divine plan.

Jesus didn't go into the wilderness because He had the idea on His own. The Father directed Him to go. The Gospel of Mark says that immediately after His baptism, "the Spirit drove Him into the wilderness. And He was there in the wilderness forty days" to fast and pray.

THE BATTLE BEGINS

It becomes apparent that a great battle between good and evil is brewing on this desolate spot as Jesus prepares for His earthly ministry. Jesus has a choice—follow God His Father, who sent Him into the world and into this wilderness, or follow Satan, who rebelled against God, the Creator of heaven and earth. Satan is there to entice Jesus to sin and change His allegiance to the spirit of darkness. The devil's highest priority was to conquer his archenemy, who had come to regain the earth for God and heaven. Would he succeed?

Satan would use his most powerful weapons to persuade Jesus to yield to his temptations—some of the same temptations he used on Eve and Adam in the Eden garden. The choices of Jesus would affect our future, and the consequence would be eternal life or eternal death. What would Jesus do under the stress of Satan's temptations?

Let's see how things unfolded. After an extended stay in the wilderness, Jesus was hungry, faint, exhausted, and full of concern for our salvation. The temptations were greater on Jesus than any temptations to sin that we have ever experienced or ever will experience. The evil one was determined to make Jesus sin so he could have dominion over the earth and prove to the universe that God's laws—His commandments—were too strict and men and women could not obey them.

TEMPTATION 1: APPETITE

Matthew 4:1–11 gives us a detailed account of three temptations. The first is appetite. In the Garden of Eden, when Adam and Eve faced the temptation to eat the forbidden fruit, they probably weren't even hungry. They were surrounded by every imaginable variety of luscious fruit and even by the fruit of the Tree of Life. But in the wilderness, Jesus fasted for forty days. As a human being in this weakened condition it was not easy for Him—His tummy was hungry like ours would be. Every cell in His body cried out for food.

Today people are accustomed to eat whatever they want, as much as they want, and as often as they want. One man bragged—"I eat only one meal a day—all day!" Appetite includes not only the things we eat, but our sexual passions as well. There is nothing wrong with eating—eating delicious and nutritious food. And there is nothing wrong with sex when shared within the covenant of marriage as God initiated this bond in the Garden of Eden. The key is self-control. Do we control our appetites, or do our appetites control us? Perhaps at no other point has Satan had so much success as he has had with the temptation of the appetite for food, sex, and addiction.

Believing that Jesus is at His weakest, most vulnerable moment, the crafty, deceitful devil seizes on the opportunity and appears to Jesus in shining white as though he is an angel sent from heaven to help him.

"It isn't God's will that You starve to death. You have power to make stones into bread. If you are the Son of God," he suggests, "make these stones into bread and eat so you won't die." The stones look like loaves. Jesus' command could transform them into real bread. Satan wants to put doubt in Jesus' thoughts. All kinds of thoughts must have splashed through Jesus' mind. But the first word—*if*— gives away to the discerning Jesus that the evil tempter is not an angel from God. Jesus hasn't come to earth to prove His identity to curious questioners, and He will not doubt the Father's care and plans for Him by taking things into His own hands.

In answer, Jesus says, "It is written, 'Man shall not live by bread alone, but by every word that proceeds from the mouth of God'"

(Matthew 4:4). The temptation was masterful, but Jesus responded with the Word of God, just as we may do when we are tempted. Where Eve had been enticed, Jesus stood firm.

In all ages, Satan's temptations that appeal to appetite—both food-related and sexual—have been most effectual in corrupting and degrading humankind. Jesus was victorious facing this first great temptation. He will help us also to be victorious.

TEMPTATION 2: CLAIMING GOD'S PROMISES WITHOUT MEETING THE CONDITIONS

Satan has more than one arrow in his quiver. "Then the devil took Him up into the holy city, set Him on the pinnacle of the temple, and said [this] to Him" (verse 5): "I'm glad to hear You quoting Scripture. I was only testing Your fidelity. I commend You for Your steadfastness and Your trust in God. I'm going to quote You the promise in Psalm 91:11, and You can show me the full trust that You have. 'He shall give His angels charge over you,' and 'in their hands they shall bear you up, lest you dash your foot against a stone.' Show me Your faith. Jump off this pinnacle. The angels will catch You."

Yes, the devil knows how to quote Scripture. He also knows how to misquote Scripture. Satan leaves out a key phrase of Psalm 91:11. After "He shall give His angels charge over you" comes another phrase: "To keep you in all your ways." Angels will keep us from falling if we are following the ways and plans of God.

Jesus answers the enemy: "It is written *again* [one Bible text is not enough—we must compare Scripture with Scripture], 'You shall not tempt the Lord your God.'" Jesus must have struggled emotionally, physically, and spiritually as He listened to Satan's temptations, so deceptively planned. There is a fine line between faith and presumption. Jesus will not jump off this high point to show His faith that God would send angels to save Him as He fell, or demonstrate His divine power by performing a miracle for His own good or to satisfy curiosity. Jesus turns His back on the second temptation. He will fight the battle as you and I have to fight it.

TEMPTATION 3: SEEKING WORLDLY GLORY

Twice Satan's temptations have been thwarted. Now the enemy carries Jesus to the summit of a high mountain. With the effect of a motion-picture panorama, in a few moments he passes before Jesus' sight the glories of all the kingdoms of the earth. They see the splendor of the sun shining on fertile fields and the sparkling glory and unsurpassed beauty and affluence of the cities. There is the gold of Caesar's palace, the treasures of Egypt, the fabulous wealth of Mesopotamia and the faraway lands of the East. Hidden from view are the wretchedness, the grinding poverty of the masses.

"Jesus," he says, "there is no need to shed Your blood to win back the world. I'll give it all to You *free*! I'll give You the riches of all the kingdoms. No pain! No sacrifice! No Calvary! No cross! I will give You happiness, honor, riches beyond imagination. Just worship me, and I will give You the world and all its glory. Just bow down and worship me, and it's all Yours!"

But Jesus shakes His head *no*! "Satan, you want proof I am the Son of God? Here it is! I command you. Away with you, Satan! Be gone! For it is written, 'You shall worship the Lord your God, and Him only you shall serve.' "

VICTORY ON THE BATTLEFIELD OF TEMPTATION

Satan is forced by divine command to retreat from the field of battle. Jesus has faced every temptation on which Adam and Eve were defeated when they surrendered the rulership of this world to the enemy. Jesus has faced the same big three temptations but under infinitely more difficult circumstances. Where our first parents fell, Jesus has been totally victorious. He has endured inexpressible anguish. Though physically weak and emotionally spent, Jesus has stood for the right and chosen allegiance to God.

Writhing with humiliation and rage, Satan is forced to quit and withdraw. Defeated, he slinks away muttering to himself, "*I'm not finished with Him yet.*" Luke 4:13 says, "Now when the devil had ended every temptation, he departed from Him until an opportune time." Christ is Conqueror.

TEMPTED JUST LIKE WE ARE

At the beginning we said that Jesus came "to seek and to save that which was lost" (Luke 19:10). He would go back to where Adam and Eve lost their way and gain the victory.

What were the temptations to which Eve yielded when she disobeyed the express command of God and ate the forbidden fruit in the Garden of Eden? Genesis 3:6 names the three temptations. "So when the woman saw that the tree was [1] good for food, that it was [2] pleasant to the eyes, and a tree [3] desirable to make one wise, she took of its fruit and ate. She also gave to her husband with her, and he ate."

It was the devil's purpose to bring about an everlasting separation between God and people. But Jesus came to earth and passed over the same difficult ground as we do. He became a part of our family and shared our same human nature. Jesus became fully human and remained fully divine. As a child and youth, His stepbrothers, stepsisters, and playmates ridiculed Him and tempted Him to react to their unkind ways. "Why won't you join us in our pleasures like all the other youth in Nazareth?" Jesus understands what it is to be mocked for standing for right principles. When Jesus hit His foot against a stone or the leg of a chair, He hurt just as we do. Jesus understands and sympathizes with our weaknesses, because He has been there—He was tempted in all points as we are. He has promised us, "Resist the devil and he will flee from you" (James 4:7).

What do these temptations and victories mean to you and me? Now, as our brother, Jesus is aware of our temptations and cares about us. He wants to help us have victory over the hurricane forces of temptations in our lives that Satan continues to throw in our daily path. As in the times of Christ, Satan the destroyer chooses to attack us at our weakest points, in a weak moment or a difficult time. Instead of being alienated from God, we become more closely united to Him through Jesus than if we had never fallen. He has bound Himself to our humanity with a tie that is never to be broken. He invites us to be members of the heavenly family. Our Jesus Brother loves us dearly and wants us in His Kingdom. When we are surrounded by temptation, He will strengthen us to say "No! No way! Be gone! I am not going that way!" When we are tempted and even when we have fallen, we can "approach the throne of grace with confidence, so that we may receive mercy and find grace to help us in our time of need" (Hebrews 4:16).

After the three temptations were over, the devil fled, and it was clear to the on-looking universe that Jesus was victorious. He was totally spent, exhausted from His weeks without food, and He fell, almost dying, to the ground. At the moment of extreme need, "angels came and ministered to Him" (Matthew 4:11). Jesus was strengthened with angel food and with the assurance that His victory was approved by the Father. What an ordeal He has gone through for us. We praise and thank Him for enduring these traumatic temptations and physical deprivation that we might have life eternal.

And today in this world, Satan keeps tempting us—promising the same to you and me: "You may have all this if you follow me."

"No thanks!" we answer. "Get away from me, Satan. I choose Jesus as the Lord of my life. I resist you, the devil." Then we draw nearer and nearer to God daily by communicating with Him in prayer and Bible study. We listen for His gentle voice: "Follow Me, and I will be with you always, until you enter the eternal home, where there will be no sin and only true, unending joy, vibrant health, love beyond comprehension. There are riches beyond your imagination waiting for you."

*Do I believe that Jesus can give me victory
over Satan's temptations?*

REFLECTION

1. This is a personal question to ponder: What are your greatest temptations? When Satan slithers into your spiritual path, how can you resist him on these points?
2. Today we face many temptations. But we face the same big three that Adam and Eve did. How can you and I claim total victory over the enemy when he entices us with sins that are commonly accepted in our culture?
3. Appetite is a temptation to many. In which areas of appetite do you have the greatest temptations? What steps are you taking to have victory over these temptations as Jesus did?
4. A religious author wrote: "Satan trembles and flees before the weakest soul who finds refuge in that mighty name [of Jesus]." What goes through your mind as you read this quotation? Do you agree? Where have you found strength to resist when assailed by an almost overwhelming temptation?

JESUS–WHO IS HE?

He is the Tempted One, the Victorious One. He is One of Us. He is the One Who Gives Us Power to Overcome as He overcame.

FROM BEGGAR TO BELIEVER

Jesus is walking into Jericho one day. A multitude on their way to the Passover celebration in Jerusalem swells the town crowd. Near the gate of the new Jericho, built by Herod and site of one of his several palaces, sits blind Bartimaeus, begging. He is there each day as the traffic goes by. Since he can't see anything, his other senses are heightened. He hears the slap of leather sandals on the road. He smells the livestock as they pass by. He feels the smooth coins people have tossed on his gray cloak stretched out on the ground before him.

This day a noisy crowd is moving along, and blind Bartimaeus senses an unusual buzz in the group. He inquires, "What's happening?"

"Jesus of Nazareth is passing by." He has heard that Jesus performs miracles, and hope springs up in his heart.

Casting off all reserve, he begins to cry out, "Jesus, Son of David, have mercy on me! Jesus, Son of David, have mercy on me!" Literally, he is calling Jesus Messiah and Lord.

"Shush! Be quiet! Stop disturbing the peace!" the bystanders scold him. But the more they reproach him, the louder he shrieks in desperation. This may be his only chance.

"Son of David, Messiah, have mercy on me!" Notice that this man in need of healing claims no merit for himself; his only claim is the mercy of Jesus.

Jesus hears, stops walking, and commands those nearby to bring the blind man to Him. His ear is always tuned when someone asks for mercy.

One in the crowd says to Bartimaeus, "Be of good cheer! Stand up! He is calling you." This is music to his ears. Blind Bartimaeus refuses to be detoured, he won't be distracted. "And throwing aside his garment, he rose and came to Jesus."

Now the two are face to face, and Jesus asks the big question: "What do you want Me to do for you?" This is also a great question for us today. Some of us would answer, "A slice of bread" or "Heal my drug addicted teen" or "Take away this headache" or "Help my husband to stop beating me" or "Show me where to get a job" or "Heal my baby." Jesus hears the cries of the sincere heart. He can discern between the cry of need and the cry of greed.

The blind man makes his request: "Lord, that I may receive my sight." Bartimaeus has a specific *felt* need. He doesn't make ambiguous, hazy requests of Jesus that are so general that he wouldn't know if they were answered or not. He says, "That I might receive my sight again."

With compassion and love, Jesus says, "Go your way: your faith has made you well." Instantly the healing miracle takes place. Immediately the blind man can see. He praises God. The people around are amazed and glorify God.

What was the key word Jesus used at the healing moment? "Your *faith* has made you well." The man believes that God will do what He promised. In a few seconds, blind Bartimaeus has gone from beggar to believer.

And whose is the first countenance that he has seen in years? The kind face of Jesus. Joy bursts out in his heart and on his lips. "And immediately he received his sight and followed Jesus on the road."

Blind Bartimaeus had lost his eyesight, but he did have insight. The sighted crowd around him did not necessarily see Jesus as the Savior of the world. Today, people have sight for material things but are blind to spiritual realities. Most do not know WHO HE IS.

God enjoys being merciful and gracious to us, not because we are worthy but because we are totally unworthy. Our only right to His mercy and kindness is our great need.

In this short story we find seven steps that will help transform your life. To go from being a spiritual *beggar* to being a *believer*, you need to:

1. Be open to new experiences the Lord wants to share with you. Listen with ears tuned, and tell God especially when you first wake up in the morning, "Speak, Lord, I am listening."
2. Recognize the Source of help: "Jesus, Son of David." Recognize Jesus as Messiah and Lord.
3. Claim no merit. "Have mercy on me!"
4. Cast off every hindrance. What could be a hindrance or distraction for you in your spiritual walk? Could there be some sinful act or habit that blocks God's desire to answer your prayer?
5. Beg for fulfillment of your felt need when the Master nudges you with, "What do you want Me to do for you?"
6. Believe and claim that God will respond to your needs. Heaven is full of miracles.
7. Follow Jesus in life's way.

What do I want Jesus to do for me?

REFLECTION

1. This episode may have been Bartimaeus's only opportunity for healing. Have you ever thought, *Tomorrow I'll call on Jesus for help. Sometime soon I'll ask Him.* Have you known anyone who waited too long and found there was no tomorrow? Reflect on what happened. How can you apply the blind man's story to your life?

2. Do you have something you want to say to Jesus, about some keenly felt needs, for example? We aren't speaking of generalities or hazy requests. If Jesus says to you, "What do you want Me to do for you?" what would you tell Him is your big need? Share your concern with someone else, and then together tell Jesus about it in prayer.

3. Do you have faith and believe that Jesus will do this for you? Would God be honored by granting your petition? Are you willing to Believe and Follow?

JESUS–WHO IS HE?

Jesus is Lord! He is the Messiah! He is the Miracle Giver! He makes the blind to see. He heals those who are spiritually blind so that they may see His tender, caring face. Jesus of Nazareth is passing by. Do you want Him to stop and call you? Do you want to follow this Jesus as Bartimaeus did?

We can cooperate with God in our healing by obeying natural law which He created—in faithful exercise, drinking sufficient water, adequate nutrition, etc. and the supernatural God cooperates with us in granting us the healing power of Love, Forgiveness, Renewed Mental Faculties for decision making in the frontal lobe of the brain, and making us a New You, etc. At times when we commend ourselves into God's hands in a health crisis, He heals us by supernatural miracle. There is a cooperation between Divine power and human effort.

All true healing—prevention and reversal of disease—comes from Jesus. Since He is the Creator God, He gave us life at birth and He can restore our lives using the health factors pictured in the diagram below. The next chapter asks the question, "Do you want to be made well?"

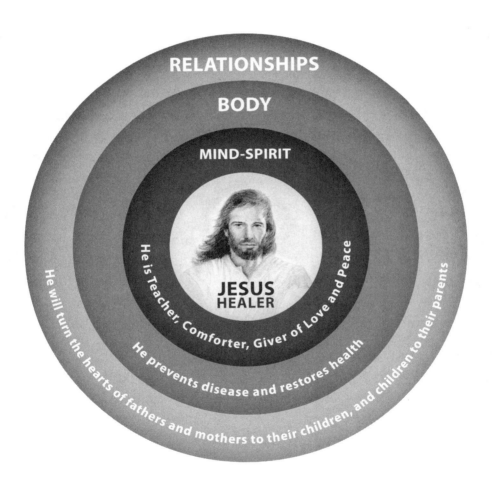

HOPE FOR THE HOPELESS

The Spanish explorer Ponce de Leon spent years searching for the legendary Fountain of Youth, supposedly a spring with magical powers that bubbled from the ground. Those who drank from it, the legend said, would be healed of any physical ailment and their bodies would once again be youthful. Sadly, he never found it.

Centuries later, not much has changed. We're still looking for the fountain of youth. Women try to find it in make-up and wrinkle-erasing creams. Men and women seek it by having their faces lifted and tummies tucked. Some lie out in the sun or go to suntan parlors so they can have that "youthful glow." A century or two ago, the goal was to become aged so that you could enjoy the respect old age brings. But today the goal is to look as young as you can so you can feel good about yourself. As much as we try, and as many breakthroughs as science hands us, our search for the fountain of youth seems to end the same way Ponce de Leon's search ended. It is forever elusive.

Jesus once met an invalid, a man whose life was like a flickering candle, about to go out in the darkness. Thirty-eight years he had waited for healing, but in vain. There was no one to help him. He had lost hope.

The crippled man had been brought to the Pool of Bethesda, a place where, according to legend, whenever the water bubbled, the first person to plunge into the water would be healed of whatever disease he might have.

One day Jesus was walking alone, apparently in meditation and prayer, when He came to the Pool of Bethesda. Under its five porches, many sick people waited for the bubbling of the water, waiting to be healed. He saw this case of supreme wretchedness, the man who had been a feeble cripple for thirty-eight years. Alone and friendless, the sufferer, feeling that he was shut out from God's mercy, had passed many years of despair there. He lay helpless and hopeless on his mat.

JESUS' MERCY

Bethesda is a word that means "house of mercy." The pool was next to the Sheep Gate, a tunnel that led into the city of Jerusalem. Here flocks of sheep were checked for quality. The unblemished sheep were accepted for sacrifice at the temple, but the blemished or defective were rejected and left outside the gate.

On this Sabbath day the crippled man suddenly looked up and saw a caring, understanding face bending over him with love and compassion.

Jesus spoke. "Do you want to be made well?"

What remarkable questions Jesus asked. On a different day, He asked a blind beggar named Bartimaeus, "What do you want Me to do for you?" as though the blind man might choose among several options. Now to the shriveled sufferer He asks, "Do you want to be healed?" What a strange question. Would the man perhaps not want to be healed? The truth is, though, that some people don't know what they want, while others enjoy the pity party of being sick.

Instead of saying "Yes," the man answered, "I have no one to help me get into the pool, and when I try to get there by myself, I've never been the first one in."

Then he heard an unbelievable command from this sympathizing Stranger: "Stand up, pick up your mat, and go home!" What do you think his reaction was? The command was to perform a task that he had not done for almost four decades—an impossible command! He could have quibbled and said, "I don't have the strength to do it." But no, a Man with the kindest face he had ever seen had commanded him, and he would do it. He willed to get up, and heaven supplied the strength. Jesus, the God of Mercy, standing in the "House of Mercy," showed Him mercy.

A miracle took place—the impossible made possible! Without doubting, the man set his will to obey the command of Jesus, and every muscle responded to his will. Leaping to his feet, he was a new man. At Jesus' command, the man's broken body was healed!

Jesus slipped away into the crowd, and the healed man, rejoicing in his newfound strength, picked up his mat, praising God, and with firm, elastic steps, headed for home. Wow! Unbelievable turn of events after thirty-eight years! What great joy to the healed and the Healer!

When Jesus looks at you and asks, "Do you want to be made well?" how do you respond? You and I are as helpless to live a vibrant spiritual life as was the cripple to stand up at the Pool of Bethesda. We can't get rid of the load of sin and guilt in our own power. But the tender face of Jesus bends over us and offers to take our sin and guilt away giving us new life. He can heal our emotions and bring healing to our body in many ways.

JESUS–WHO IS HE?

Jesus is the great Healer. In Exodus 15:26 God says, "If you diligently heed the voice of the LORD your God and do what is right in His sight, give ear to His commandments and keep all His statutes, I will put none of the diseases on you. . . . *For I am the* LORD *who heals you."*

In Jeremiah 30:17 the great Healer promises, "I will restore health to you, and heal you of your wounds." And, of course, today we need not only physical but emotional healing. The Master says in Isaiah 61:1, 2, "The Spirit of the Lord God is upon Me. . . . He has sent Me to heal the brokenhearted . . . to comfort all who mourn." What mat are you lying on? A philosophical mat of complacency or indifference to others around you? Maybe it's the mat of guilt or shame, the mat of un-forgiveness, hatred, malice, unhappiness, misery in your marriage, or the mat of substance abuse. Maybe it's the mat of pride. Do you think it's time to get up from that mat and be healed?

Do I want to be made well?

PREVENTION AND HEALING OF DISEASE

Scientists tell us that the Prevention and Healing of Disease takes place at 3 levels:
1. Primary Prevention. Someone who is apparently healthy. Preventing risk factors from developing.
2. Secondary Prevention. Managing Risk. Reversing the risk factors of high blood pressure, high cholesterol etc., and preventing them from becoming disease.
3. Tertiary Prevention. Reversing Disease. Helping the body heal itself. The individual may already have heart disease, nerve or kidney damage, etc., but healthful living may prevent progression. We avoid those things that tear down the body, and make sure we're taking in enough of those things that build up the body. Harness God-ordained remedies by optimizing positive forces at work (exercise, nutrition, water, adequate rest, etc.) and minimizing negative forces (addictions, improper diet and beverages, etc.).

God works at all 3 levels. He works in vitalizing the lifestyle, preventing disease and its complications. When we have done all we can at the natural level, Jesus can intervene at the supernatural level as we have faith in him, just as He did for the crippled man at the Pool of Bethesda. Jesus said to the former cripple later when he met him in the temple, "See, you have been made well, Sin no more, lest a worse thing come upon you" (John 5:14). So the Bible teaches that even after a miraculous healing, the healed person has the responsibility of changing his/her lifestyle so as to not fall back into the same or worse disease.

Henry Ford said, "Whether you think you can or you think you can't, you're right." There is Somebody bending over you whispering, "Do you really want to be made well?" Do you want to be made well more than you want harmful addictions and habits that are increasing your risk factors for disease and a short life span? It's your body. You decide! You can do the impossible if you connect with the Source of power.

REFLECTION

1. Do you feel blemished and defective, shut out from God's mercy and healing, His love and protective care? Why do we continue to suffer with guilt and sin? You can look to the risen Lord and say, "I accept the power to do the impossible that only You can give. Forgive me of my sins; set me free; heal me." Is that your decision?

2. Do you think that the power to get well is just in some magic phrase that a healer repeats? Is the power inside of you? Or is the power in God's promise that becomes yours when you believe it?

3. Someone once said, "When we pray for healing, God *always* answers our prayer. In some cases there is instant healing. In other instances the healing is a gradual process. Or perhaps God sees that our greatest need is emotional or spiritual healing rather than physical. Or healing takes place emotionally, spiritually in the family. Sometimes the healing

will come when with glorified bodies we ascend to heaven. But God always answers the sincere prayer for healing." Do you agree?

JESUS–WHO IS HE?

He is the great Healer! Psalm 103 says: "Bless the Lord, O my soul; and all that is within me, bless His holy name! Who forgives all your iniquities, who heals all your diseases." Do you want to be both forgiven and healed? What is your response?

THE IMPOSSIBLE IS POSSIBLE

I lived a pretty rough life. I'm sorry to tell you, but I indulged in many sins. I didn't always obey the rules I was brought up with. My motto was, "*If it feels good, do it! If it tastes good, eat it!*" Although there were momentary thrills, I found no lasting satisfaction.

Then the dreaded paralysis hit. None of the pleasures of my fast life were important to me anymore. Grandma still tried to take care of me. To my surprise, one evening my last four friends came over—the rest had long since gone their own way. They said, "Good news! Jesus has come to town."

"Jesus? Who is He?" I asked.

"He's the One who is healing all the sick people! Haven't you heard?"

"Oh yes," I said, "I guess I've heard about Him. But I doubt He would want to heal me. I'm a sinner. The church people around here won't even pray for me. They tell me that my paralysis only serves me right. It's divine payback for how I've been living for the past twenty years."

"Good news!" my faithful friends said. "We're going to take you to Jesus right now. He's teaching over at Peter's house."

As I lay on my stretcher, unable to walk, my skin shriveled, my face already carrying the paleness of death, my thoughts vacillated between believing and doubt. The enemy whispered to me in my mind, *It's no use, there's no hope for you.* But then I felt my stretcher go airborne as eight strong arms hoisted it to their shoulders, and we were heading down the street to the center of town. Peter and his family lived a short distance from the church.

When we got there, it seemed as though the whole town was gathered at Peter's door. My four friends called out, "Please let us through! This sick man needs to get to Jesus. Please let us through!" But even near the door, the people were packed in tight. Everyone was trying to hear Jesus. No one budged an inch. Then an idea hit me. *It seems hopeless here. Let's try the roof.*

It was a balancing act trying to keep me from falling off as they struggled with the stretcher up the narrow outside stairs. Once on the roof, I could hear my friends taking off the tiles. Now I could hear Jesus' melodious voice as He spoke to the people in the crowded room below. They tell me that everybody looked up surprised as the meeting was interrupted by bits of mortar and tile falling from above—especially the church leaders and the lawyers on the front row. Yes, everybody except Peter. They tell me that Peter looked truly astonished—he couldn't believe what was happening. After all, it was the roof of his house.

The church leaders brushed the debris off their clothes and tried to rub the dust out of their eyes. And the people who wouldn't budge before now pushed back, pressing against each other. Nobody wanted to have my heavy stretcher land on his head. And my four friends? They were up above, holding ropes that let me down gently into Jesus' presence—right in front of Him.

As Jesus watched the drama unfold before His eyes, He looked at me tenderly, with sympathy in His eyes, and said, "Son, your sins are forgiven." Really, it was forgiveness I wanted. I had been a very sinful person. And now I lay there in perfect peace. I felt that I could die knowing my sins were forgiven. I was free from the shame and guilt of a great many sins! All I could say was, "Thank You, Jesus!"

Then I heard Jesus say, "So that you may *all* know that I have the authority to forgive sins, I say, 'Get up! Take up your cot and go home to your wife and family!' "

Suddenly I felt a strange sensation flooding my body, the thrill of new life washing through my veins. My nerves and muscles, which were shriveled and useless from my numerous strokes, suddenly felt sensitive and strong. I sensed that feeling was restored to the left side of my body. It was like being shocked by an electrical current. I looked at my hand, and it was pink with perfect circulation. I jumped to my feet, turned around, and burst into tears of joy and thanksgiving. I was healed! I was healed!

From the bottom of my heart I said, "Thank You, Jesus!" Then, with bouncing steps, in obedience to the forgiving Healer's command, I picked up my tattered cot and headed for the door. The packed crowd miraculously parted, and I walked through as the people stared at me in awe. Joyfully walking past the people who earlier refused to give us entrance, I heard them saying, "We have seen strange, amazing things today."

And my four friends? As they drew up the rope from the roof, they shook their heads. What seemed impossible, Jesus had made possible.

A few minutes later, as I went through the door of my humble house, my wife, your grandma, stared at me with a look of complete disbelief. I gave her the first two-armed loving hug I had been able to give her for years, kissed away her tears, and then kissed and hugged each of our children as I said, "Jesus made all the difference! He forgave my sins! He healed me!" That night, melodies of happiness and praise ascended to heaven from our little home.

Blessed are the desperate! For they will tear the roof off if necessary. They will gladly give up dignity for an encounter with Deity. If the occasion demands it, they are willing to be unconventional. They are willing to climb a sycamore tree. They are willing to burst into Jesus' presence even if they are untouchable lepers. They will break through cultural barriers and claim crumbs from the Master's table. They will let Jesus put mud into their eyes, and they will jump into a pool at the Master's command. Blessed are the desperate! They will not argue about what God does or how He does it.

In the story of the healing of the paralyzed man, it is natural to focus on the man himself. However, one phrase in the narrative puts a different twist on the story: "When Jesus saw *their* faith"—that is, the faith of the four stretcher bearers as well as the paralyzed man. The forgiveness and healing of the paralytic was the result of the faith of all five! Theirs was a prayer of agreement.

Jesus promised, "If two of you agree on earth concerning anything that they ask, it will be done for them by My Father in heaven" (Matthew 18:19). Better yet if there are five of you!

Forgiveness is important in the healing process even today. Jesus is both the *Forgiver* and the *Healer*. Forgiveness usually precedes healing. When Jesus takes my guilt away, every nerve and cell in my body senses the peace that is beyond understanding. And as the negativity and corruption are siphoned off by the blood of Jesus, I can *arise*. This word spoken by Jesus to the paralytic is the same word Jesus spoke to Jairus's twelve-year-old daughter who was dead. *Arise!* And so the resurrection miracle of life is mine. I can sense a new life and a new purpose in life. I am forgiven! I am healed!

You and I have been paralyzed. Our mat may be the mat of subconscious shame, and our paralysis guilt. Jesus came to take away that mat. No human being or human method can take away the consciousness of sin. It can't be done by yoga or meditation or by an earthly priest, rabbi, or pastor. We don't need to work ourselves into a trance; we just need to come to the same Person who healed the paralytic. He is the Forgiver—the Healer.

And the forgiven will be forgiving. Forgiveness is my willingness to release someone who has wronged me, and although the wrongdoer may still have to pay a debt to society, I leave him or her in the hands of God. True forgiveness is the beautiful fragrance that the flower sheds on the heel of the one who crushes it.

Can Jesus forgive all my sins and mistakes and heal me?

REFLECTION

1. Luke 5:17 says that teachers of the law and religious leaders from many faraway cities were present when the miracle of the healing of the paralytic took place. They were the scholars of the time. Then the verse says, "And the power of the Lord was present to heal them." Why is it that although learned men and possibly hundreds of people were packed in and around Peter's house, only the paralytic is mentioned as being healed? The power of the Lord was present to heal them all. Why weren't many others healed? Why not everyone?
2. Has anyone, like the paralytic's four friends, been encouraging you? Is anyone praying for you? Are you willing to pray for someone else who may be having a tough time? Share your story.
3. The big point of the paralytic's story is that Jesus forgives sin. Micah 7:19 says that Jesus "will cast all our sins into the depths of the sea." And then He puts up a sign: "No fishing allowed here." Are you willing to let Jesus bury your sins in the sea of His love?

JESUS–WHO IS HE?

He is the Forgiver, the Healer. He gladly forgives when I don't deserve it. He longs to accept anyone for whom friends are hanging in there and praying them through a crisis. Have you accepted and claimed His forgiveness? James 5:16 says, "Confess your sins to one another . . . that you may be healed."

BROKENNESS TO WHOLENESS

8

The girl with the cover-girl face and covered-up life, as Dwight Nelson puts it, approaches the ancient well with her water pot. All the other women come on this errand in the early morning or evening, but the girl with the cover-girl face and the covered-up life comes to the well at scorching midday to avoid disdaining glances and unkind jabs from the neighborhood gossips.

A Jewish stranger is sitting on the mossy lip of the well. She acts as if she is unaware He is there. After all, isn't it a rule that Jewish men don't talk to women on the street, especially if she is from a despised race like the Samaritans?

As she lowers and then raises her goat-hair rope, drawing the filled water pot to the top of the hundred-foot-deep well, she clutches the jar and is about to leave when the stranger surprises her by asking, "Would you be so kind as to give me a drink?" Her curiosity is aroused that He would ask a favor from a woman of a despised race.

She questions, "You, a Jew, are asking me, a Samaritan woman, for a drink?"

He replies, "If you only knew the gift God has for you and who I am, you would ask me, and I would give you living water" (John 4:10, NLT).

Jesus, the Stranger, continues as He points to the well, "Everyone who drinks this water will get thirsty again and again. Anyone who drinks the water I give will never thirst—not ever. The water I give will be an artesian spring within, gushing fountains of endless life" (vv. 13, 14, MSG).

Thinking that He's referring to physical water, she says, "Sir, give me this water so I won't ever get thirsty, won't ever have to come back to this well again!" (v. 15, MSG).

Jesus gazes into the pretty face and knows that behind her pleasant mask is a woman with desperate spiritual needs. And so He looks into her eyes and says, "I desire to give you living water. In fact, I want to provide it to you and your husband, so go home and bring him to Me." He is leading this woman to face up to her past but also to the amazing fact that in spite of her past, God is still willing to give her living water.

"I have no husband," she replies.

"You've had five husbands, and the man you're living with now isn't even your husband. You spoke the truth there, sure enough," Jesus says (v. 18, MSG).

THINK ABOUT IT

Like the woman of Samaria, you may long for Living Water. Is there a desert in your life? Are you thirsty? "The water I give will be an artesian spring within, gushing fountains of endless life." "Come! And let him who thirsts come."

Jesus, who knows every detail of our lives, does not reproach her for the immoral conduct of having lived with five different men and living with another one in the present. Instead, He offers her something better. The woman recognizes her spiritual need and, that very day, accepts Jesus as the Water of Life. Here is water—pure, refreshing, artesian, and eternal.

Dwight Nelson writes,

> *Living as you and I do in a world of parched, painful dreams and brittle, broken lives, wouldn't it be the height of insanity for us to cling to our cracked cisterns and broken water jars while Jesus stands before us, beckoning us to a gushing spring of living water? His offer isn't only for her!*

Jesus also calls us to that gushing spring of living water. He says, "Let anyone who is thirsty come to me."

AN EVER-FLOWING ARTESIAN SPRING

James Wilson of Kent, Washington, needed more water for his five-acre tract of land. He hired a professional well-digger, and they chose a spot behind the Wilson home where they hoped to find water. They began to sink a steel shaft into the earth. Slowly the work continued. Fifty feet, a hundred feet, a hundred and fifty feet through earth and then rock. No water!

"Shall I continue?" the well-digger asked.

"Yes!" replied Mr. Wilson. "We must have water." As the drill crunched its way to 210 feet (64 meters), they heard a faint sound from far below. It quickly became a gurgling sound of rushing water. The two men stepped back just in time as a geyser shot up with unbelievable force into the sky. Abundant gushing water—they got it!

They called neighbors with shovels to dig drainage ditches, but that was not enough. Someone brought a backhoe, but that was not enough. The next day, heavy equipment from the county road department arrived to try to channel the flood. The operators dug ditches that could bring irrigation to the entire valley. Geologists arrived and estimated that water was spouting out of the ground at a rate of 1,600 gallons (6,056 liters) per minute. That was enough water to supply the needs of a city of 46,000 people! They had created an artesian well that was ever flowing.

Water is essential to life. It quenches our thirst and helps the body to function properly. Birds, fish, animals, plants—all living things must have water. Human beings can only live a few days without it. A proper level of water in the body helps maintain the correct acid-alkaline balance and furnishes the vital current that carries nutrition and oxygen to every cell of the organism. Our brain is about 75 percent water, and if water is scarce, the brain progressively loses its cognitive powers. Water is also called the universal solvent. It cleanses the body of toxic chemicals. It cleans us inwardly and outwardly.

In the Bible water symbolizes the essential spiritual cleansing that we all need. Baptism by water is a heavenly ordained symbol of being buried in the likeness of Jesus' death, and then being resurrected to a new spiritual beginning to walk in new life.

The cover-girl woman with the covered-up life found an artesian well that met her every need, that flooded her soul with life-changing power.

KARL HAFFNER SHARES A BAPTISM STORY

"Excuse me, pastor," the young woman said as she tugged on my arm in the crowded church lobby. "I want to be baptized."

"Praise the Lord," I said. While her face looked familiar, I didn't even attempt her name. "That's wonderful. Um, I'm sorry, I should know you but—"

"Oh, I'm Candie. I've been coming to your church, and I would like to become a Christian."

"Great! Let's meet this week to make the arrangements."

Later that week I reviewed the basic doctrines of our church with her. She was obviously well studied and conversant in Christian beliefs. As part of the review, I mentioned the concept of spiritual gifts. "For example," I said, "one of my gifts is teaching, so I don't mind talking in front of people."

"I think that's my gift too," she said.

"Really?" I tried to disguise my surprise. "Well then, um, would you be willing to say a few things at your baptism? Right before I baptize you, I'll ask you to share your story of how you came to Christ. Would you be comfortable with that?"

"Sure."

Sabbath morning I stood with Candie in the baptismal tank. She was prepared to tell her story.

I, on the other hand, was not prepared for her story. I knew nothing of her background. Nor did I anticipate her testimony.

Her opening words quieted the hushed noises in the sanctuary. "I was a teenage prostitute and worked for twelve years as a stripper."

I had never seen the church members so attentive—certainly not during any of my sermons. My pulse doubled as I wondered where her story was going next.

I marveled at how poised Candie could be. Her sordid saga unveiled the seediest shadows of society. But she didn't dwell there. Instead she spoke of the amazing grace of God. I affirmed in my mind her intuition that indeed she had a gift for public speaking.

"But that's all behind me now," she concluded. "I am going to leave that old person at the bottom of this tank. God tells me that I will arise a new creation. If God's grace can cover me, then there is no such thing in God's vocabulary as an ineligible candidate. If God can change me, He can change anybody. Praise God for His incredible grace."

With that, I momentarily buried Candie in Christ's death. As she exploded out of the water with resurrection power, the church members applauded for what seemed like fifteen minutes.

Later, I couldn't find Candie at the luncheon that we hosted in her honor. "Have you seen Candie?" I asked several people. Nobody had seen her. At last I discovered her sitting alone in the sanctuary by the baptistery.

"Hey, Candie," I said, "you OK?"

"Oh, pastor, yes! I've never been better. I just wanted to watch all my sins go down the drain. I can guarantee that this baptismal tank will never hold as many sins as it did today. For the first time in my life, I feel clean!"

In that holy moment it hit me with fresh force—the power of God to forgive and transform a sinner. Only God can change a prostitute into a promise-keeper. Only Christ can reconstruct the composition of a human heart. Only He can stoop into the shadows and salvage the brokenness of a spiritual casualty like Candie. Or you. Or me.

Lest you think Candie's story is any different than yours or mine, may I remind you that we all stand as moral and spiritual failures in the baptismal tank. It is only by God's cleansing grace that we can find forgiveness and freedom from our sins. All we have to do is acknowledge His grace and accept His gift.

Can I, with my sinful past, find healing of my emotions and a new life of purity—a new beginning?

REFLECTION

1. The mission of Jesus was "to heal the brokenhearted, to proclaim liberty to the captives." How did Jesus set these two women free?

2. What do the two stories say to you?
3. Jesus, who knows every detail of our lives, does not reproach the immoral conduct of the woman of Samaria. Why not? Didn't she deserve to be reproached?
4. How do we deal with someone who has made mistakes because of human weakness? Should we condemn the fault or offer something better?
5. Who is happier: (a) a proud, accepted man who doesn't think he has sinned, or (b) a fallen person who finds the way back, depending only on Jesus? Which person makes heaven more joyful? (See Luke 15:7.)
6. (Personal reflection—do not share publicly.) In your repentance process, you may wish to confess specific sins to Jesus so that you can be fully cleansed and start a new spiritual journey.

_____

_____

_____

JESUS—WHO IS HE?

Ask the woman of Samaria. He is the Living Water. He washed away my sordid past. He made me a new person—innocent, clean, joyful. He can do this for you too!

(This chapter is based on the story found in John 4).

9

JESUS—AT MY HOUSE?

Only minutes after Jesus healed blind Bartimaeus, He and the multitude pressed on into Jericho. In that town, one of the chief agents for tax collecting, a man named Zacchaeus, wanted to see Jesus. The town was only a short distance from the Jordan River, and Zacchaeus had probably been one of the thousands who flocked to the Jordan to hear John the Baptist preaching some three and a half years before. On one of those occasions he might have heard John say to the tax collectors, "Collect no more than what is appointed for you" (Luke 3:13). Fraud and overcharging were rampant among the Jewish businessmen who worked for the Roman tax office. No accountability plan was in place, and they could charge whatever they wanted to the populace. As long as they themselves paid the required quotas to the Roman authorities, they could pocket all of the difference. If there was any trouble collecting, the tax collectors had the support of Roman soldiers.

Zacchaeus didn't feel good about himself, but he thought that money would make others look up to him and help him have a better opinion of himself. So he plunged into practices of exploiting the rich and the poor. Zacchaeus was the moral and functional equivalent of what today we call a "repo man," who makes his living by repossessing cars, houses, or other items used as collateral for debt. His version was to take your donkey, your ox, or your sheep. He would take your last pigeon that you needed for a sacrifice at the temple in order to cover the tax you didn't have enough money to pay. Zacchaeus' bank account grew, yet happiness eluded him. Something was missing.

Zacchaeus had decided to change his financial behavior and had already begun to give some of his goods to the poor and to restore what he had wrongfully taken. He was haunted by the hollowness of his life. Word had gotten around that Jesus offered hope to the worst of sinners and that He had even chosen a tax collector as one of His disciples. Maybe there was hope for Zacchaeus too. If only he could find forgiveness of his past and peace in the present! It would take a miracle to turn his life around. Zacchaeus could not purchase with money what he needed in order to find peace for his soul.

The sun is shining brightly on that early spring day. It gets brighter yet as word spreads that Jesus is coming into town. There in Jericho, Zacchaeus wants to see Jesus. Light from the Sun of Righteousness is beginning to beam into his heart.

But the tax man has a problem. He is short. He cannot see over the bobbing heads and waving hands of the multitude. Jesus is advancing down the street. Zacchaeus can hear the acclamations, but, even standing on tip-toe, he can't see Jesus. Laying aside any thought of what people might think of him, he runs ahead and grabs the lower branches of a sycamore fig tree. Shimmying up to the tree, he finds a perch on a limb overhanging the street and says to himself, *Now I can see Jesus, but Jesus will probably not see me up here*. He is determined and desperate. He must see Jesus.

He is in for the surprise of his life.

The crowd finally comes near the fig tree. Jesus stops, looks up among the leafy branches, and calls him by name!

"Zacchaeus, make haste and come down, for today I must stay at your house." Jesus has come to save the whole nation—the whole world—yet He comes to this man's house!

As Jesus steps over the threshold of Zacchaeus' stately home, He announces, "Today salvation [healing of brokenness] has come to this house." Zacchaeus is so moved by Jesus' offer of friendship that his mind is immediately made up. He determines to complete the change of habits he began three and a half years before. His conscience has bothered him so many nights, and he has sensed guilt so many days! His heart is swelling up inside of him, and he realizes the pain he has brought on himself as well as others and that his lavish home isn't as important as inner peace. Deeply moved, Zacchaeus repents of his dishonest past and makes a new resolution to help the poor. That is his prayer.

RESTITUTION IS PART OF RECOVERY

The nonprofit organization Alcoholics Anonymous incorporates restitution and making wrongs right into its Twelve-Step Program. Included in the twelve steps are:
- Make a list of all persons we have harmed, and become willing to make amends to them all.
- Make direct amends to such people wherever possible, except when to do so would injure them or others.

When the gospel goes to work on his heart through the power of the Holy Spirit, it cannot be business as usual for this businessman. We find Zacchaeus awakening to the fact that business carried on without integrity and fairness is bad business in the sight of God. But he does not leave this as just an idea. He begins to take action to rearrange his business affairs and practices. When he meets Jesus, Zacchaeus makes three final decisions:
1. To give half his income to the poor
2. To restore four times as much to those he had cheated to make sure he had made everything right
3. To break his addiction to moneymaking.

He decides that he isn't the ultimate owner of his material blessings, rather God is the real owner of the world and everything in it. He is only a steward, appointed to care for some of God's resources until the Lord should ask for it back.

Some people probably despised him still, either because he was turning his back on fortune-making or because they couldn't forget the overcharging and fraud he had practiced in the past. But Jesus said, "Today salvation has come to this house."

JESUS—who is He? Jesus is salvation. When you accept Jesus into your home, you accept salvation.

Notice that this divine gift was not only for Zacchaeus but for his whole family also. Does it make a difference when Jesus comes to our home and dwells with our family? A few years after Jesus met Zacchaeus, the apostle Paul, on one of his missionary journeys, experienced an earthquake that opened the doors of the prison in Philippi, where he was being held. The keeper of the prison asked Paul and Silas, " "Sirs, what must I do to be saved?" The answer came,

" 'Believe on the Lord Jesus Christ, and you will be saved, *you and your household.*' . . . He rejoiced, having believed in God *with all his household*" (Acts 16:30, 31, 34, emphasis supplied).

When parents give their hearts to Jesus, does it influence their home life and their children? Yes, it does. The Bible tells us the story of a youth named Timothy whose family lived in Lystra, in what is now the country of Turkey. The mother, Eunice, was a devoted follower of Christ, as was the grandmother, Lois. Although the father was not a Christian, there was a heavenly atmosphere in this home, and young Timothy became a devoted follower of Jesus. Timothy accompanied Paul on his missionary journeys as Paul's closest co-worker. The faith of the grandmother and mother became the faith of young Timothy.

During most of Jesus' life up to the age of thirty, He lived with Mary and His stepbrothers and stepsisters in Nazareth. His siblings did not accept Him as the Savior of the world. But at the Passover in AD 31, His siblings saw Him die on the cross. We don't know the subsequent history of all of them, but James and Jude accepted Jesus as their Savior and later became pillars in the church and contributors to the New Testament books of the Bible. It makes a great difference when Jesus lives in your house.

Zacchaeus received Jesus into his house, into his family, and into his life. He repented of his past. His priorities changed. Now it wasn't about how much he could *get* but how much he could *give*. Money was a resource to be shared with those less fortunate than himself. Zacchaeus learned that money doesn't make you happy, but spent carefully and generously with the worthy poor, and given liberally to support the sharing of the gospel, it makes both you and others happy.

Do I want salvation to come to my home and family?

REFLECTION

1. What does the Zacchaeus story say to you and to your family?
2. Is it your desire to have Jesus come to your house? What might you do to bring Jesus in so that salvation comes to your family, whether they live at home or are away from home?
3. Think through your life. Is there anyone who needs a restoration gift from you?
4. In what ways might relations have improved in the community after Zacchaeus restored funds and gave to the poor?
5. Jesus called Zacchaeus by name, even though they had never met before. Does Jesus know your name? Why do you think so?
6. How would you feel if Jesus offered to come to your house right now? Imagine that He came and knocked at your door. How would you react?

7. Jesus knew that Zacchaeus needed Him. He was a social outcast, isolated from the majority of people in the community. In prayer, tell Jesus what your desire is—for Him to come to you or not to come.

JESUS–WHO IS HE?

Ask Zacchaeus. Jesus is salvation. This day Jesus brings salvation to my house. He is the Giver of Repentance to cleanse of past sins. He is the Restorer. He crystalizes my plan to restore all dishonest gain and to help the poor and needy.

(This chapter is based on the story found in Luke 19:1-10).

RICH BUT POOR

Besides meeting Zacchaeus, Jesus met another rich man who lived in that region. He is commonly known as the Rich Young Ruler. During the final weeks of Jesus' ministry, as He was journeying toward Jerusalem and the cross that awaited Him there, He traveled in the province on the east side of the Jordan River. Mothers had brought their children to have this renowned teacher, Jesus, put His hands on them and bless them, but the disciples reproached the mothers and sent them away. Jesus called the mothers back and gathered the little children in His arms and blessed them. The Rich Young Ruler saw the children give to Jesus wild flowers they had picked along the road, and he saw the smiles on the faces of the careworn mothers.

Although this ruler usually felt little concern for mothers and young children, he had watched the episode from a short distance away. As Jesus got up and started on His way to the south again, something stirred within the heart of this young man. He, too, wanted a blessing and assurance that all was well with his soul. The Bible record says, "Now as he was going out on the road, [he] came running, knelt before Him, and asked Him, 'Good Teacher, what shall I do that I may inherit eternal life?' " (Mark 10:17).

Who was this young man? He wasn't a casually interested person. He came *running*. He was in earnest. We don't know his name, but many believe he was one of the seventy members of the Sanhedrin, the ruling assembly of the Jews. The twelve disciples looked at this illustrious young man, and Judas may have thought, *At last we are going to get followers who are rich, who will bring money into the treasury. It's about time!* The young ruler had a huge estate, well-built barns filled to overflowing, and extensive, rich farmlands. To human eyes, he had it all!

The record in the book of Mark continues on a tender note. "Then Jesus, looking at him, loved him." Jesus saw the young man's almost infinite possibilities. He was intelligent and learned. He could have been one of the authors of the Gospels. He could have been a leader in the early Christian church. The young ruler could sense the warmth of love that radiated from Jesus toward him.

He had asked Jesus what he could do to inherit eternal life. Now came Jesus' reply.

"One thing you lack: Go your way, sell whatever you have and give to the poor, and you will have treasure in heaven; and come, take up the cross, and follow Me." Jesus was saying, *Your wealth doesn't ultimately belong to you. God lends it to you to help the helpless, the poor, and the hungry, and the needs of extending God's kingdom. It's OK to have a well-built home like Peter or Matthew have in Capernaum. But beyond your frugal living expenses, share with God's children even as God has shared with you.*

The face of the young ruler fell. If he had been living today, we might say he ran through his mind the last balance sheet brought up the night before on his computer. What does he love the most? His huge assets in the stock market and real estate, or Jesus and the kingdom? The biblical narrative closes with the grim words, "But he was sad at this word, and went away sorrowful, for he had great possessions."

EXCESS WEALTH BRINGS WORRY
SHARING YOUR RICHES BRINGS JOY

Karl Menninger, co-founder of the Menninger Clinic in 1925, came to be known as the "dean of American psychiatry."

Dr. Menninger was asked what a person should do if he felt a "nervous breakdown" coming on. He said: "Lock up your house, go across the railroad tracks, find someone in need, and do something for them."

"Some don't dare give, they might run out. My dear friends, of course you are going to run out. You can't take it with you. I don't know how many hundreds of my patients are now asleep in their graveyard, leaving behind far more money than they could handle, far more money than their children could peacefully divide."

Let's use a little imagination and make up the rest of the story. Some thirty-five years go by. The Rich Young Ruler is no longer young. His hair has turned gray, and his face bears the wrinkles of age. He has added to his estate and built new and bigger barns. His spacious home is the envy of the community. But then the Roman-Jewish war of AD 66–70 breaks out. Tens of thousands of Roman soldiers sweep through the land, pillaging, killing, burning, and destroying everything. The great estate that rich ruler had been unwilling to share with the poor and helpless, he sees going up in flames. He sees the soldiers coming toward his house, spears in their hands. He thinks back to the distant past, when, on the road not far from his home, he had run to Jesus and asked Him what he could do to inherit eternal life. Had he made the right decision thirty-five years earlier?

What am I willing to give up to follow Jesus?

REFLECTION

1. What does the story of the Rich Young Ruler say to you?
2. Who do you think made the best long-term investment, Zacchaeus or the Rich Young Ruler? Why?
3. In chapter 9 we studied about Zacchaeus. Would you rather be a Zacchaeus, a Mrs. Zacchaeus, one of the short little Zacchaeus children, or would you rather be the Rich Young Ruler, Mrs. Ruler, or the children of Mr. and Mrs. Ruler? Why?
4. The young ruler was rich. Was he really poor? Explain.
5. A famous hymn says, "I surrender all." What are you willing to surrender to Jesus?

JESUS–WHO IS HE?

Jesus is the Inviter. The Rich Young Ruler would say, "He invited me to come and follow Him." How do you respond when Jesus invites you to share what is valuable to you, take up your cross, and follow Him? Are you impressed that Jesus is inviting you and your family on a spiritual journey?

LOST AND FOUND

11

Mothers and sons, fathers and daughters. Jesus understands relationships. A family and their relationships is one of the most touching stories Jesus ever told (Luke 15:11–32), a rich father has two sons. The younger son says, "Dad, I want my inheritance now." Usually the estate would be divided at the death of the father and mother, but this young son is not patient and does not want to wait. He wants it now.

The son is eager to leave home. The far country is calling—calling him to be free, to do whatever he wants. The voice in his head says, "You will be happy, successful, have power to climb to higher levels of popularity and prosperity, to be rich and famous. You can do things your own way—have no restrictions and have freedom from responsibilities." The voice calls him to do things that may not be part of God's plan for him. He wants liberty to go on his selfish fantasy search. He tells his father, "Dad, I just want independence— to be on my own. Give me my part of your money and let me go."

Then the father does the unexpected. Without scolding his son, he exchanges land for gold and silver and, in boundless love and mercy, consents to the request and gives this demanding son his share of the inheritance, knowing that it is not for his best good but respecting his son's freedom of choice. The defiant son receives that which he has no right to.

The son does not become lost in the far country but chooses to become lost even before he leaves. He is deaf to God's plans for him and ignores the still small voice of the Father. He doesn't want to follow the heavenly rules—God's commandments and family laws. He chooses Eden's apple of death and not the promise of eternal life. This persistent son is now his own boss. He thinks he is free! The son is loaded down with gold and silver coins, but he will eventually carry a much heavier emotional load.

With the inheritance money in hand, the son leaves for the distant city. Today, it could be Las Vegas or New York. Perhaps Paris or Bangkok. Maybe his destination would be a tropical beach in Rio de Janeiro.

Arriving at the far country, the Prodigal thinks, *Victory at last! I'm going to enjoy the life here. I'm going to make it big. I will become rich, famous, and powerful.* Now it is party time with new friends the father would not approve of. He throws lavish parties for new acquaintances, and the girls flock around him. They welcome the wealthy newcomer to the far country.

The son begins to spend money extravagantly on fancy clothes, fellow pleasure seekers, and on the best lodging to impress others. He makes friends who gather around him with open hands. He is now free to do what he wants, and happy to be disconnected from home and spiritual values.

But the young adventurer is a walking dead man. Yes, he still moves, but his conscience seems dead. He hasn't taken time to communicate with God or attend religious services. He is ruled by his passions. His motto is: "Eat, drink, and be merry. Live it up! Do what you want!"

Finally, though, a disturbing reality begins to set in. The funds are dwindling, spiraling down day by day with wasteful spending. The bank account gets close to zero. The prodigal son has tasted everything he hoped for, lots of luxury, great food, many friends, and a lavish lifestyle, thanks to his father's generosity.

One night he is with a group of his wild friends, treating them to fine vintage wine. When it's time to pay the bill, he reaches into his moneybag and discovers he does not have enough funds. The money is almost gone!

His "friends" take off immediately, as though he is a case of the plague. Today we might say that he has to give up his luxury hotel room that night and, for a few nights goes through the shock of having to sleep in his heaviest coat in an alley, near a sidewalk grate. Perhaps he applies for government help, but they tell him that as a foreigner he is not eligible. He has no money to even buy a meal. He has to go to work, but the only work opportunity is feeding pigs in a pig pen. He gets so hungry that he is ready to eat pig food.

Sin had deranged his thinking, compromised his will-power, rendered him incapable of reasoning throughout his downward spiral. But now he hits rock bottom and "comes to his senses." He thinks, *Hey, I'd be better off as a servant at my father's home than I am here!* In desperation he decides to leave the far country and head for home. He should return with generous gifts for his family, but he is penniless, and that is out of the question.

On the way he prepares his speech, rewording it over and over in his mind. "Father, I've sinned against heaven and against you, and I'm no longer worthy to be called your son. Make me one of your servants. I don't expect you to have me as a son. I'm happy to work as a slave."

Unknown to the son, day after day, year after year, the father has been looking down the path that leads up the hill to his house, hoping and praying that his lost son will reappear. He loves him dearly. Then one day, the father sees a lone figure in the distance. *Can it be? Yes, the walk is like his long lost boy!*
It must have been quite a scene. The father running down the hill

shouting, his servants running after him to see what is the matter! An ecstatic father kisses his dirty son; he hugs him tight before he can speak. The son is barefoot, his clothes are rags, his face thin and haggard—but the father's eyes see his own flesh and blood returning home. With open arms he receives his son, and they cling to one another in a teary, lingering embrace.

The son begins his prepared speech: "Father, I have sinned against heaven and against you, and I am no longer worthy to be called your son. Make me—" But that is as far as he gets. The father interrupts him by calling the highest-ranking servant.

"Bring out the best robe and put it on him, and put a ring on his hand and shoes on his feet. Quick! Get a banquet ready. It's time to celebrate, for this my son was dead and is alive again; he was lost and is found!" His son is overwhelmed. He can't speak. His rags are exchanged for a robe—the best robe. The father commands his servants to dress the son as they would a king.

Psychiatrists have found that there is tremendous power in persisting, unrelenting parental love. Immature adolescents and young adults learn from what their parents do and are, not so much from what they say. Sometimes bad behavior is a teen's way of asking, "Do you really love me?" They want to know if you only love them if they do everything your way. What you *do* carries more weight with them than what you *say*.

Jesus says there is "joy in heaven over one sinner who repents." (Luke 15:7). Sometimes we only think about the things that make us happy. But could we do something that would make God happy?

Notice the wonderful, gorgeous robe provided to the son. The robe is a gift, unasked for, freely given. The lost son didn't earn the robe or pay for it. He didn't deserve it. His father freely gave it.

Friend, that's what the Father God does for each of us. Maybe we have wandered to the far country and done much to hurt ourselves. Our heavenly Father is a great Giver of blessings, and yet if we waste them, squander and misuse them, finally they are gone. But that great loving heart draws us back home.

In this story we see that God's love allows us to make choices, even if they are not good for us. We may choose to cut our relationship with our Father God. Yet, He remains the Father and His love continues to be persisting and unrelenting. If our eyes could be opened, we could see the Father waiting for us to come home.

Does God still love me even if I have done many sinful things?

REFLECTION

1. Where are the voices calling you to go? What are they telling you to do in your far country of life?
2. What are some of the spiritual implications that surface in this story of the Prodigal Son who wants to go to a far country?
3. Did the lost son earn the pure, clean robe he received? Was it given because of his good works and personal merits? If not, on what basis did he receive it?
4. Is there anything you can do on you own that's good enough to give you perfect standing before the judgment bar of God?
5. Right standing before God means that you accept His change in your life on your behalf. Do you want God to do something for you that you can't do for yourself? What is it that you want God to do for you?

JESUS–WHO IS HE?

The Amazing Jesus is the White Robe Giver who offers a clean robe to you as a free gift. Would you like to say this? "Thank You, Jesus! I accept the pure, white robe You have graciously provided me. Thank You that I can come home again like the lost son and be part of our loving Father's family."

12

MY JOURNEY TO JOY

The apostle Paul tells the dramatic account of his meeting with Jesus

The amazing JESUS—WHO IS HE? I can tell you from my experience, because I met Him. Even though He no longer lived on the earth, I saw Him with my own eyes. The scene dazzled my sight and blinded me on the Damascus Road. Now, thirty-three years later, I stand to defend my divine encounter and my friendship with Him.

Let me share my present circumstances. I am on trial before the emperor again. I have to wonder what Nero sees when he looks on my face. Here I am, a man aged prematurely, of slight stature, stooped from the heavy burdens I have borne so long. My eyes are very bad. When someone takes down a letter for me, I can hardly see to write my name at the end of it. I, Paul, stand here a prisoner for Christ before the highest tribunal and the most absolute tyrant in the world.

What brought me here? After my final missionary journey came to an abrupt end in AD 67, the authorities sent me to Rome to face Nero for the second and final time. I am accused of instigating the burning of Rome, a crime that apparently Nero himself committed. It has been approximately five years since my first appearance before the emperor. In my first trial before him, the charges were treason, heresy, and sacrilege. The judicial decision: no crime proven, no case for Roman jurisdiction. I was acquitted. I had spent two years incarcerated in Rome awaiting my first trial. But as I wrote to my friends, "I want you to know, brethren, that the things which happened to me have actually turned out for the furtherance of the gospel" (Philippians 1:2).

In my second trial, I once more have the opportunity to lift up the banner of the cross before a wondering multitude. As I gaze upon the throng before me—Greeks, Romans, Jews, strangers from many lands—my soul is stirred with an intense desire for their salvation. I lose sight of the grave occasion, of the perils surrounding me, of the terrible fate that seems so near. I see only Jesus, the Intercessor, pleading before God in behalf of sinful men. With more than human eloquence and power, I, by the grace of Christ, attempt to present the truths of the gospel. I point my hearers to the sacrifice made for the fallen race. I declare that an infinite price has been paid for the human race's redemption. Provision has been made for them to share the throne of God. By angel messengers, earth is connected with heaven, and all the deeds of men, whether good or evil, are visible to the eye of Infinite Justice.

I am expecting to be sentenced to death. However, I refuse to allow my thoughts to spiral downward into the abyss of despair or despondency. In fact, "I am now ready to be offered, and the time of weighing anchor is at hand. I have fought a good fight, I have finished my course, I have kept the faith" (2 Timothy 4:6, 7, author's translation).

I think back on my early life and how good God has been to me. My life began in the Gentile city of Tarsus in Cilicia. My father was of the tribe of Benjamin and a Pharisee. Because of my birthplace, I was born with Roman citizenship. In an earlier defense of myself before fellow countrymen in Jerusalem, however, I had pointed out to them that even though I was born in Tarsus, I was "brought up" in Jerusalem, learning at the feet of the renowned teacher Gamaliel. I became a Pharisee myself, and the most dedicated kind at that. I was ready to persecute and kill the "enemies" of our religion.

Having heard that some of our "enemies," the followers of Jesus, had fled to Damascus, I set out on a trip there to track them down. As my small entourage and I journeyed on horseback, we followed the road as it descended from the desolate Syrian mountains, and there our eyes feasted on the fertile lands, beautiful gardens, and a fruitful plain with the spires of Damascus beyond. In my pride I exulted that I was carrying documents from the high priest that authorized me to enter the synagogues in Damascus and arrest any Jesus sympathizers I might find and bring them in chains to Jerusalem for trial, imprisonment, and perhaps death. It might well be that after completing this mission I would be appointed as a member of the Sanhedrin.

As we rode along, suddenly a dazzling light shone right into my eyes—brighter than the noonday sun. The light was too glorious for mortal eyes to bear. Utterly blinded and bewildered, I fell to the ground. I heard a voice saying, "Saul, Saul, why are you persecuting Me?"

I stuttered my response, "Who-who are You, Lord?" I had a sneaking suspicion whose voice I was hearing.

The voice answered, "I am Jesus, whom you are persecuting."

The men in my entourage saw the light and heard a voice, but only I understood the words. These words struck home to my heart with devastating force. The current of my whole life changed instantly, when I met Jesus on the Damascus Road.

My "conversion" was not typical in any way. In fact, I must say truthfully that I was called against my will (1 Corinthians 9:16). I did not volunteer for service. No, Jesus Christ Himself interrupted me in my pursuits in a dramatic and forceful way. But from then on, "I was not disobedient to the heavenly vision" (Acts 26:19).

As I reflect on my current predicament, permit me to remind you what the gospel of Jesus Christ is all about. I believe the letter the

Holy Spirit guided me to write to the Romans is an appropriate synthesis of the gospel. It most fully explains my journey to joy.

I state my basic proposition in the letter to the Romans, chapter 1, verses 16, 17: "I am not ashamed of the gospel, because it is the power of God that brings salvation to everyone who believes: first to the Jew, then to the Gentile. For in the gospel the righteousness of God is revealed—a righteousness that is by faith from first to last; just as it is written, 'The one righteous will live by faith.' " Essentially, then, my joy arises from the fact that the power of God is revealed through the gospel for all who have faith.

I had been raised in my religious culture to believe that my salvation depended on the good deeds I did. I was trying to work my way to heaven. But after I encountered Jesus on the Damascus Road, I learned that my salvation depended on my believing and accepting what Jesus did for me on Calvary. "God demonstrated His love and grace for all of us in that while we were yet sinners Christ died for us" (Romans 5:8). "Nothing can separate us from the love of God in Jesus" (8:39).

Based on my message to the Romans, here is the good news of the gospel.

1. Righteousness, or right standing before God, is "apart from the law" (Romans 3:21), which means it is not earned by law keeping.
2. Instead, salvation comes "through faith in Jesus" (Romans 3:22)—by believing that what He has promised is true and is for us.
3. Since all have sinned (Romans 3:23), all deserve death (Romans 6:23).
4. God does not give us the death we deserve, but rather what we do not deserve, the free gift of grace (Romans 3:24), which we accept by faith.
5. This gift is available because of Christ's death on the cross. His sacrifice not only pays the penalty of our sin, but it provides

for us *redemption* (a word meaning "buying back a captive"), and *justification* (a word meaning "to count as righteous"), and *reconciliation* (a healing of relationships), and *cleansing* from the pollution of sin.

6. All this is made possible by the blood of Christ. In other words, Christ died the death that was ours that we might have the life that was His.

7. The enemy Satan whispers to us that this gift of right standing before God really can't be for us because our sins are too bad. If we accept the enemy's whispers, we make God a liar. Yes! God's promise is true, and we can claim it, not someday but right *now*. At this moment, by the blood of Christ, we can stand before God clean and pure, as though we had never sinned. Why? Because God says so, and His pledged word is true!

If some of my words are not in your everyday vocabulary, let me explain more simply through what I wrote to the Ephesians:

God is so rich in mercy and He loved us so very much, that even while we were dead because of our sins, He gave us life when he raised Christ from the dead. (It is only by God's special favor that you have been saved!) For He raised us from the dead along with Christ, and we are seated with Him in the heavenly realms—all because we are one with Christ Jesus. And so God can always point to us as examples of the incredible wealth of His favor, and kindness toward us, as shown in all He has done for us through Christ Jesus.
God saved you by his special favor when you believed. And you can't take credit for this; it is a gift from God. Salvation is not a reward for the good things we have done, so none of us can boast about it. For we are God's masterpiece. He has created us anew in Christ Jesus, so that we can do the good things He planned for us long ago (Ephesians 2:4–10, NLT).

Having right standing before God becomes effective the moment a person puts her or his faith in Jesus Christ and accepts Him as Savior. It is a present status enjoyed by believers. So we can say, "Therefore, since we have been justified through faith, we *have* [present tense] peace with God through our Lord Jesus Christ" (Romans 5:1).

I have been forsaken by my friends, as you may have been. Some friendships don't pass the test of persecution. My friend Demas stayed with me when it was popular to be my co-worker, but when I was accused unjustly of serious crimes, he abandoned me. On the other hand, as a young man Mark couldn't take the hardships of travel in robber-infested territories and left me to return home to Jerusalem on the next ship. But later he wrote the Gospel According to Mark, and I sent for him to help me in my ministry again. He is now a tried and tested, self-sacrificing disciple.

The one Friend who never forsakes us is Jesus. He stood with me as I defended Him before Nero in the highest court of Rome. As I said after my first trial, "Notwithstanding the Lord stood with me, and strengthened me; that by me the preaching might be fully known, and that all the Gentiles might hear: and I was delivered out of the mouth of the lion. And the Lord shall deliver me from every evil work, and will preserve me unto His heavenly kingdom" (2 Timothy 4:16, 17).

I have carried out my mission in the eastern Mediterranean "through the power of the Spirit" (Romans 15:19). I have followed Jesus in my journey to joy. "Jesus—who for the joy that was set before Him endured the cross, despising the shame" (Hebrews 12:2). I too am finishing my race with joy.

Now I can hear the cadence of synchronized footsteps as the Roman guards approach to take me away. Under a military escort, I will be executed beyond the city walls, on the southwestern side of the city, on the road that leads to Ostia, the port of Rome. Because I am a Roman citizen, I cannot be crucified. I will be beheaded.

But the promise is mine. "There is laid up for me a crown of righteousness, which the Lord, the righteous Judge, shall give me at that day: and not to me only, but unto all them also that love His appearing" (2 Timothy 4:8).

How do I have contentment and joy in all circumstances of my life?

REFLECTION

1. What does this topic of Paul's journey to joy say to you?
2. When forsaken by a friend, how do you react? How should you react to this painful experience?
3. From his prison in Rome, Paul writes, "Rejoice in the Lord always. Again I will say rejoice!" (Philippians 4:4). "Yes," he says, "I am being poured out as a drink offering on the sacrifice. . . . I am glad and rejoice with you all" (Philippians 2:17). If Paul is joyful and glad even under persecution and imprisonment, how can we find lasting joy in our journey on the upward way?

BECOMING A MARTYR

Might it not be the lesser of two evils to compromise and worship the statue of the emperor, rather than leave your children without a parent and your spouse without a bread winner? This was the decision Christians were forced to make. Peter, Paul, James—indeed all of the 12 apostles except John were martyred. Peter was crucified in Rome. His dying wish that he be crucified upside down was granted. Peter, who had denied Christ 3 times during Jesus' trial before Caiaphas, counted it too high an honor to die in the same way as his Lord. Tradition says that John, author of the book of Revelation and the Gospel of John, was thrown into a caldron of boiling oil, but that his life was preserved and the same executioners finally had to take him out. Tradition says that Thomas went to Chennai India, where the Thomas Christians still exist. He was killed with a spear.

But even martyrdom has no merit in and of itself. St. Paul, taught that motivation is everything. In 1 Corinthians 13 he says, "though I give my body to be burned, but have not love, it profits me nothing."

Tertullian said, to the Roman governor of his province in North Africa in the 2nd Century, "The oftener we are mown down by you, the more in number we grow; the blood of Christians is seed." These words have been paraphrased to say, "The blood of the martyrs is the seed of the Church."

The blood of the martyrs is the seed of Christianity, if we love Jesus. He died for us, and if duty so calls, the highest honor would be to die for His cause. So the question in early times was "Confess or deny?" Confess that you are a follower of Jesus, or deny that you are a Christian.

Jesus said, "Whoever confesses Me before men, him I will also confess before My Father who is in heaven. But whoever denies Me before men, him I will also deny before My Father who is in heaven" (Matthew 10:32, 33).

JESUS–WHO IS HE?

He is the Amazing Jesus who appeared to me, Paul, on the Damascus Road. He is the One who transformed me from persecutor to persecuted. He chose me. I count it an honor to die for Jesus, even as He died for me. For to me to live is Christ, and to die is gain. I long for the resurrection when my Journey to Joy will be realized in the joyous presence of my Lord and Savior, Jesus Christ. My fellow pilgrim, will you today make Christ part of your "journey to joy"?

13

THE DECISION THAT CHANGED THE WORLD

As the reader may have discovered, there is a gigantic war between forces of good and evil being waged in this world. Occasionally we catch a glimpse of the unseen forces and their strategies. An angel who witnessed the Garden of Gethsemane conflict, might report the merciless battle transpiring that night, ushering in Good Friday some 2000 years ago.

After supper, shortly before midnight, Jesus and eleven disciples, His friends, leave Jerusalem through the Fountain Gate. The city is hushed. I see them walk past grape vineyards, cross the Brook Kidron and climb part way up the Mount of Olives. The moon shines full as Jesus and His friends make their way to the Garden of Gethsemane, which means "oil press". Here is a hillside olive grove where Jesus often went for prayer, but never before with such a heavy heart. He knew He had to make an extremely difficult decision.

I see Jesus exceedingly sad and unusually quiet this night as He laboriously walks with His friends to their place of prayer. Near the garden entrance, Jesus tells eight of the disciples to wait; He then proceeds into the deeper recesses of the grove with Peter, James, and John. I hear Jesus solicit His close friends, "Stay here. Be in prayer with Me?"

The tone of His voice seems to be saying, *I need your prayers. The next few hours are going to be extremely difficult for Me and for you.* Many times Jesus has spent entire nights praying here for others—

but this time is different. He feels the need of having Peter, James and John spend the night in prayer with *Him*. Why? Jesus senses a horror of darkness coming. He needs their sympathy, concern and love. Did His friends not know what was going to happen in a few hours? We angels knew Jesus came to be humanity's Substitute in death, to carry the burden of all the sins for a lost world. God made Jesus, who did not commit any sin, to be sin for them (humankind) (2 Corinthians 5:21).

Now the hour of decision has come. It is the crisis hour; the fate of Jesus, the fate of the universe, and the fate of each individual human being's eternal destiny are in peril. He must not fail. We angels know this is the crucial moment. Will the blotch of sin remain forever in the universe, or will Planet Earth be reclaimed so that one pulse of harmony may beat in all God's creation? This night the decision will be made.

It is evident Jesus is in deep emotional and physical pain. He is weighted down and overwhelmed by the enormity of sins upon Him. Troubled and deeply distressed, Jesus says to his close friends, "My soul is exceedingly sorrowful, even to death. Stay here and watch" (Mark 14:34). Jesus asks Peter, James, and John to watch and pray because He knows they too will be severely tempted. We angels see Jesus withdraw a short distance to be alone; He must fight His own personal battle in this great conflict. Struggling to walk, Jesus falls on the dew covered ground and in agony cries out loud to His Father God, pleading: If it is possible let this cup pass from Me.

I see Peter, James, and John pray for a time, but overcome by drowsiness, they fall asleep. In agonizing prayer, Jesus, with groans, pours out His soul to His Father. Will the sins of humankind separate Him from His Father? Jesus knows if He is to save all from eternal death, there is no way for Him to escape the dreaded darkness ahead of Him. Jesus came to earth for this purpose. In order to serve as humankind's Substitute, He has to accept a painful withdrawal from His Father.

The sins of the world disconnect Jesus from the perfect communion and unity He has had with His Father. Jesus will have to make this decision and face its consequences all alone—can He? Adam failed the test of sin; now Jesus must be the Victor. Will His human nature endure the atrocities Satan is ready to inflict? Jesus conquered Satan's temptations in the wilderness. With Calvary looming, can Jesus conquer sin for all eternity? I see His body trembling in agony as He pleads with God. Oh how much we angels would like to help Him, but the Father instructs, "No, not yet."

Satan appeals to Jesus with a final and forceful arsenal of temptations. Satan desires to overcome Jesus at this crucial decision time. The conflict is horrendous. There is no turning back, no escape. Consequences of failure are unthinkable—Satan would be victorious, and the world would become his dominion to rule forever. The enormities of humankind's sins are crushing the life from Him. I see, as the Savior lays His hand on His chest. His heart must be physically aching. He pleads with God for strength to endure the crisis. He has lived His life in close communion with His Father, and He dreads the conflict ahead when He will be separated from His Father God. His closest friends are not there to provide support and love, but rather I see Satan's evil angels surrounding this sacred spot. My fellow angels and I raise our hands resisting the demonic host lest they attempt to physically overwhelm the Savior.

How does Jesus pray? The Bible tells us, "In the days of His flesh, when He had offered up prayers and supplications, with vehement cries and tears to Him who was able to save Him from death . . . though He was a Son, yet He learned obedience by the things which He suffered" (Hebrews 5:7, 8). Now tears crease the Judean dust running down Jesus' face. In anguish He prays more earnestly.

It is blackest night, but more than physical darkness surrounds Jesus. Later we angels learned that before the sun went down the next day, Jesus endured seven mock trials, was scourged or physically abused six times, was nailed to a cross until His death, and was buried in Joseph's new tomb. He suffered the second death—the death of eternal separation from God, the type of death unsaved people will suffer at the end of time.

Jesus' grief is beyond comprehension, as nothing I have ever seen. The Father does not respond to Jesus' pleading. This path is trod alone. The cumulative weight of the world's sin, including yours and your families', is placed on Jesus. He is the Divine-human sacrificial Substitute for sinful transgressors. Jesus seems to be in excruciating pain as He senses the Father's presence being withdrawn. Father God is separating Himself from sin. From Jesus' anguished lips, a deep-hearted prayer wells up, "*Abba* [Daddy], Father, all things are possible for You. Take this cup away from Me, nevertheless, not what I will but what You will" (Mark 14:17).

I've witnessed so many times what sinners think of sin. For many of them, sin is an enjoyable pastime; millions think nothing of a 'small' transgression here or there. Many individuals seek and relish a life separated from God. To Jesus, however, sin is hateful, painful, and the most damaging thing in the universe. For Him, innocent of any sin, to carry all the sins of the world unto eternal death is abhorrent. Yet, the Savior willingly takes these sins onto Himself.

As human beings we long for sympathy in suffering. Jesus is no less human; He covets sympathy and support during these extremely heart-wrenching moments. He desires support from close friends, His cherished companions for the past three and a half years. After an hour of wrestling in prayer, I see Jesus return to Peter, James, and John. Are they pleading for Him in prayer? No, Jesus finds His friends overcome by a strange stupor, sleeping. Jesus knows what is coming this night; He knows His close friends need to pray for protection from evil, both for themselves and for Jesus. Peter, James, and John will be targets of forthcoming temptations. Jesus is concerned and wants to shield His friends from the evil that soon will overtake them. When Jesus wakes them up, they cannot find words to excuse their behavior. Christ knows that this very night, His dear friend Peter will deny that he even knows

Jesus. Peter will need supernatural power to overcome Satan, so Jesus directly addresses him.

"Peter, could you not watch with Me one hour? Watch and pray that you enter not into temptation."

SWEAT OF GREAT DROPS OF BLOOD

Bloody sweat is a rare medical condition known as hematohidrosis. It happens when, under severe stress, the blood leaves the capillaries and goes into the sweat glands and is excreted through the pores. This usually happens when the individual is at the point of death from terrible anguish.

With excruciating pain Jesus staggers back to His secluded garden retreat. In agony of soul He wrestles again in prayer. The physician Luke writes, "His sweat became like great drops of blood falling down to the ground" (Luke 22:44). Again the Savior prays the same words, "O my Father, if this cup cannot pass away from Me unless I drink it, Your will be done" (Matthew 27:42). The olive and cypress trees are silent witnesses, dropping cold dew on the prostrate form of Jesus; nature herself is weeping with its Creator.

Again I see Jesus returning to His friends, the disciples, seeking prayer support. Awakened, they see His disfigured face, His anxious brow stained by blood. Jesus gently admonishes because He loves them: *"Watch and pray that you don't fall into temptation."*

A third and final time, Jesus struggles to His secluded, sacred spot to communicate with His Father. Jesus implores with agony and tears, pleading for strength to face the imminent onslaught. While men sleep, I see Satan pull out all the stops. Satan knows that if Jesus conquers, then he, Satan, will lose his dominion of this earth in the great controversy between good and evil. Everything is at stake for the devil, for God, and for all humanity. I see Satan, the enemy, urging upon Jesus the futility of dying to save others.

Your own disciple Judas has betrayed You, and Your closest disciples will abandon You. Few have accepted You, and fewer still will recognize the gift of life You intend to give. Let the whole ungrateful crowd suffer the consequences of their own sins.

We angels anxiously watch the conflict between good and evil on this never to be forgotten dark Friday morning. Our eyes are opened to see Satan's evil tormenting Jesus. It is warfare—the greatest battle ever fought. The enemy draws near trying to convince Jesus that dying is not worth the personal humiliation, the disgrace and pain. The destiny of the human race hangs in the balance, and Jesus knows the stakes. He dreads the coming atrocious cruelty and inhumane treatment instigated by Satan. We angels watch this horrendous conflict of good and evil play out in dreadful darkness; we want to comfort our dear Jesus whom we love, but we cannot. Jesus prays the third time, "O My Father, if this cup cannot pass away from Me unless I drink it, Your will be done" (See Matthew 26:44). Alone He fights the battle against Satan, the Prince of Darkness. All heaven watches breathlessly. Jesus makes His final decision. The sacred moment comes when Jesus recalls the past sinful world. He remembers how destructive sin was and is, and how millions need Him to wipe their sins away. He chooses to pay the painful price and redeem an unsaved lost world. He chooses the bloodstained path to Calvary. It's the only way Jesus can show lost human beings how much He loves them.

In excruciating agony and painful separation from the Father, Jesus stands firm. He *will* pay the price to redeem all men and women. He *will* endure all pain, suffering, and humiliation. He *will* go to the cross alone. Regardless of how many or how few accept the blood of His sacrifice for human sin, Jesus has *determined* to go through with the redemption plan made with His Father before the foundation of the world.

Having made the greatest decision in the history of the universe, Jesus falls dying to the ground. The Father God sends the highest Angel, Gabriel, to intervene and strengthen Him for the awful hours ahead. Satan's plans will be unmasked for the universe to witness. Wicked men will fulfill their purpose in cruelly and publically murdering the Son of God on the cross.

Calvary is less than nine hours away. Jesus grasps the reward of eternal life for millions of sinners—for you and yours.

"Jesus—who for the joy that was set before Him endured the cross, despising the shame" (Hebrews 12:2). "And He shall see the travail [labor] of His soul and be satisfied" (Isaiah 53:11, KJV).

THE OLIVE PRESS

Olive presses in those days had a large rock wheel that moved within a carved-out, circular rock base. This turned on an axle connected to a yoke, which was pulled by an animal. The rock wheel crushed the olives to a pulp that was put into baskets and then weighted down with heavy rocks until the pure olive oil oozed out into a vat.

Thank You, Jesus, that in Gethsemane, the place of the Oil Press, You were willing to be crushed and weighted by the sins of the world so that You could share the oil of joy (Isaiah 61:3) with all Your children who are willing to accept it.

Is Jesus with me in my dark valley of decision?

REFLECTION

1. Recall the events of this story. What are they? Repeat them in your mind to yourself—retell the story to someone—share the details with friends or in a group. Why was it difficult for Jesus to make the decision to die for all of us sinful people?
2. How do you personally relate to this story?
3. Recall the time when you first heard about Jesus and decided to follow Him. Share with someone that special time.
4. Think of a time when you personally fought a battle to do good and everything seemed to be against you. Tell how you felt.

5. Have you ever been tempted and needed friends to pray for you like Jesus did in His garden of prayer? Share with someone.
6. Have you ever had to make a difficult decision that was for the good of others but was difficult for you? In which ways did Jesus help you make the right decision and gave you the strength to do what was right.

Physical and mental fitness will support us when making difficult decisions. Jesus made the difficult decision that changed the destiny of the world. Choosing between right and wrong can be difficult. Your brain's frontal lobe, the control center, can be a sharp and clear discerning decision-maker if a healthy lifestyle is maintained. Decisions, decisions, difficult decisions. Will I choose to live healthfully or will I just do what many in my culture are doing?

Jesus decided to carry your sins and mine, even unto death. Have I decided to follow Him and care for the body He has given me? Have I decided to keep my mind in top shape to be a victorious decision-maker in troublous times? Do I accept this Jesus and plan to live eternally with Him?

JESUS–WHO IS HE?

Jesus is the Dauntless Decision Maker and Victorious Pray-er. He decided to accept the death that was yours, so that you might have the life that was His. Do you accept His death for you? His Gethsemane prayers opened the door of salvation to you and to a lost world. Do you accept the life that was His and can now be yours?

EARTH'S DARKEST DAY

The disciple John tells the crucifixion story

I, John, called the "Beloved", now regret my sleeping on that night in Gethsemane's garden. My eyes just would not stay open. I should have been there to comfort, sympathize and pray with Jesus when He was so intensively praying. The difficult decision Jesus made alone on that night long ago was heart breaking. Yet, He willingly made this decision for me and all other men and women.

TOMB OF THE HIGH PRIEST

The tomb of the Caiaphas family was discovered by archaeologists in November 1990. Construction workers building a road to link eastern and western Jerusalem accidentally broke into the burial cave. The bones of twelve people were found inside. One of the skeletal remains was of a man about 60 years old, found in a limestone box called an ossuary. The box was ornately decorated and presumed to be the final resting place of Caiaphas, as testified by the Aramaic inscription of his name on the side of the box.

After Jesus made this great and difficult decision, impacting all eternity, He went forth calmly to meet the mob that came seeking Him. The high priest, Caiaphas, was closely following Judas, the betrayer. Initially an angel appeared between Jesus and the group of Roman soldiers, priests and mob and they all fell in fear to the ground. As the angel presence disappeared, the soldiers, priests, and mob struggled back to their feet. During this time it would have been easy for Jesus to escape, rather He chose to let Himself be bound.

I was surprised at what was happening, as were my fellow disciples. Peter suggested we should escape while we could or we might be arrested too. It was a mistake to leave the side of my Friend Jesus. Now I felt guilty at my cowardice. Peter and I learned Jesus had been taken to the high priest's court, so we went there. In this place we could watch the religious trials of Jesus.

It was extremely painful to see Jesus struck by one of Caiaphas' attendants. Peter grimaced; when those standing near Peter saw his body language, they questioned him. Was he also Jesus' disciple like me? Poor Peter said, "I don't know the Man!" I shockingly watched as Jesus turned from His persecutors and lovingly looked at the denying disciple. Jesus' face held no reproach, only love. Peter's heart was broken when he realized what he had done. Peter left the judgment courtyard weeping bitterly, wandering aimlessly until he found himself again at Gethsemane's garden. Throwing himself down at the spot where only hours before Jesus had sweat blood in prayer, Peter repented of his cowardly acts. The look of love in Jesus' face could not be denied or forgotten.

Pain filled me as I watched Jesus roughly shifted from judge to judge—Annas, Caiaphas, a select Sanhedrin group hastily called in the night, to a formal Sanhedrin after dawn! I wondered why Nicodemus and Joseph of Arimathea, members of the Sanhedrin, who sympathized with Jesus, were not called. The end result of four Jewish and three Roman "judicial proceedings", a contradiction of terms since there was no semblance of justice, found Jesus guilty. He who came to the earth only to seek and save the lost was cursed by those He tried to bless.

PILATE–THE ROMAN GOVERNOR

For centuries Bible critics claimed Pilate never existed. This abruptly changed in 1961 when archaeologists found a limestone block in Caesarea Maritima at the ancient Roman theater with the inscription, "TO THE DIVINE AUGUSTUS TIBERIUS PONTIUS PILATE, PREFECT OF JUDEA HAS DEDICATED". This is in harmony with John 18 and 19. Although Pilate sought to placate the Jews by authorizing the crucifixion of Jesus, Pilate soon lost his governorship, was exiled to Gaul [France and nearby countries], and died a suicide in AD 37/38. Who was this Jesus? Are we sure He ever existed? There is now no reasonable question of the historicity of the two principal figures in the trials of Jesus—Caiaphas and Pilate.

My heart was broken as I witnessed Pilate's soldiers cruelly scourging Jesus' with whipcords. The cords had metal tips on the end that shredded my Friend's back. The soldiers ridiculed the thought that my Jesus was a King; they slammed a crown of thorns onto His head. Blood raced down Jesus' face, along with tears down my face. He was mockingly dressed in a royal purple robe. Finally the soldiers seized my precious Friend, bruised and bleeding, removing Him onto a balcony so the crowd could see. Pilate, in some way, hoped such abuse would awaken human sympathy for Jesus. However, for me to see my loving, gentle Friend being tortured with such cold-hearted inhumanity was exceedingly painful. This was the Man who healed the broken hearted and the diseased; He was the One who had willingly associated with individuals whom society had thrown away. Jesus had treated all with equality, kindness, and justice. Now He was treated exactly the opposite. People whom He had treasured brought false accusations, cursed, and spit on Him. Why would the men and women Jesus loved so much act in such a despicable rejecting manner?

Pilate, knew Jesus was innocent of all charges. Pilate's beliefs were unwittingly stated when he presented Jesus to the crowd,

"Behold the Man!" I, John, one of His disciples, have witnessed Jesus' life for three and a half years. I've seen Him raise the dead, give sight to the blind, and heal the lepers. I can testify that He personifies all the positive traits of true manhood—strength, loyalty, and love for others. Yes, He is the real Man—the God Man. Behold Him. He stands without a rival throughout history.

Trying to save his position and respect as a ruler, Pilate is on the verge of making the biggest mistake of his life. He is wavering between duty and expediency. I saw a messenger rush through the crowd, onto the balcony, and hand a letter to Pilate. I learned afterwards that the letter was from Pilate's wife Claudia, a granddaughter of Caesar Augustus. The letter said: "Have nothing to do with that just Man, for I have suffered many things today in a dream because of Him." Pilate mentally wrestles with his dilemma; his body language giving his torment away as I watch. Finally, he turns to the multitude and says, "What then shall I do with Jesus?" What a question! This question hit me in the face. What should I do? Today, I ask you the same valid question asked on that fateful Friday. What should you do?

The people standing next to me shouted out as if demon possessed, "Crucify! Crucify!" The frenzied crowd pick up the chant, shouting in an almost deafening roar "Crucify! Crucify!" The lacerated and bleeding body of Jesus brings forth no call for justice or even human pity. Pilate vacillates.

Now the chief priests make their final accusation. "Jesus claims to be a King. If you don't crucify a rival king to Caesar, you yourself are fomenting rebellion and you are no friend of Caesar!" Pilate does not deviate from his stance and repeatedly declares Jesus innocent. But the crowd isn't interested in guilt or innocence. They are thirsting for the blood of Jesus.

How can Pilate satisfy the crowd and still maintain some semblance of justice? I watch in anxiety what is going to happen.

Then, Pilate has an idea, an avenue of responsibility escape. *On this most important holiday of the year, the Passover, it is customary to release one prisoner by executive clemency. I will let the people themselves choose between freeing Barabbas or Jesus. Everybody knows Barabbas is a violent criminal and murderer, the crowd will certainly choose to free Jesus.* Smart idea, Pilate. Right? Wrong!

The chief priests run among the rabble shouting "Barabbas", and the people choose to free Barabbas. Barabbas is an Aramaic name that literally means "Son of the Father." He had claimed to be the Messiah, leading an armed revolt against Rome. He was a false Christ and a murderer. Pilate could have presented any of the three prisoners slated for crucifixion that day. He brought out the most ruthless and corrupt one. The people chose Barabbas. My head throbs with the in unison chanting of the mob. "Free Barabbas! Crucify Jesus! Away with Him!" I feel in my heart I have the same choice to make. Will I choose Jesus or Barabbas to be in my life? Will I select a Friend and Healer or a liar and murderer?

Pilate calls for a basin of water, and I saw him wash his hands. I heard him say, "I am innocent of the blood of this just man." Even though I see Pilate wash his hands, I am thinking, *cleansing your hands in water can't wash away the stain on your soul.* Pilate has participated in the perverting of justice and delivering to death the only perfect man in the history of the world! My heart cries out, *have I done this to Jesus also?*

I watched as Jesus was roughly pushed and shoved out of Pilate's judgment hall. The three-hundred-pound cross, which had been prepared for Barabbas was put on Jesus' shoulder. My beloved Friend had been denied all sleep, food or drink since the evening before. I remember now the wonderful evening when I sat next to Him, eating our last supper together before going to the garden to pray. Since then Jesus had been subjected to seven judicial proceedings and abusive floggings. The physical abuse occurred at least six times, including being crowned with thorns and beaten by angry soldiers.

Jesus' human nature could bear no more. He fell fainting beneath the heavy cross. What were the executioners going to do? No Roman soldier would degrade himself by carrying the cross. It seemed that no Jew would want to defile himself because touching something unclean would not permit him to partake of the Passover.

At this precise moment I saw Simon the Cyrenian. He was coming into Jerusalem from the countryside. He was an African from Cyrene [modern Libya]. Simon hears the foul epithets and ridicule being hurled at this innocent Man. Simon, not a believer in Jesus, even though his sons are, has a heart that is touched with pity as He sees Jesus, hungry, thirsty, and bleeding. Now Simon alone speaks up in defense of Jesus. Simon's "penalty": "You there! You carry the cross!" the Roman soldiers commanded. Why didn't I step up and carry the cross of Jesus? How I regret not taking action when Jesus needed me. Until his dying day, Simon guarded the treasured memory. He had carried Jesus' cross for Him to Calvary.

"FATHER, FORGIVE THEM"

When the execution crowd finally arrived at Calvary, I saw the soldiers violently stretch the limbs of my loving Jesus on the cross and hammer six-inch tapered iron spikes through His tender wrists and feet. When the soldiers came to the two thieves they wrestled and cursed their tormentors, but Jesus uttered the first of His seven sayings on the cross. "Father, forgive them, for they do not know what they do" (Luke 23:34). Matchless, incredible love! No one has asked for forgiveness, but Jesus offers it anyway.

I, John, searched in the crowd until I found Mary of Nazareth, mother of Jesus, crying and heart-broken. Helping her to lean on my shoulder I brought Mary to the foot of Jesus' cross. Although suffering the most intense pain, Jesus' eyes locked on His precious mother. Caringly He said, "My Mother, behold your son!" Then He looked at me and said, "John, Behold your Mother." I clearly received and accepted this Divine message of trust; from that day until the day Mary died, I cared for her. Even during Jesus' dying hours He obeyed the fifth of the Ten Commandments. In love Jesus honored His widowed mother who now was experiencing the death of her firstborn Son.

It was almost 3:00 p.m. when I heard Jesus cry out with a loud voice, "My God, My God, why have You forsaken Me?" (Matthew 27:46). In Gethsemane Jesus had carried the sins of the world, and after His third prayer of complete surrender to the Father's will, He fell dying to the ground. The angel Gabriel appeared strengthening Him and encouraging Him that He would have victory over the forces of evil. But now hanging on the cross He isn't crushed by the physical pain, but by mental and emotional anguish as He bears the full weight of the sin of the world, and because of the curse of that sin the Father must hide His face from His own Son. Could it be that Jesus suffered the same penalty that the wicked will finally bear—sensing eternal separation from God?

A moment before Jesus died, I heard Jesus' triumphant shout resounding through the earth and it must have echoed through heaven and worlds afar.

"It is finished!"

I didn't understand the full meaning of those words then, in fact my heart was torn asunder, but over the years the meaning has become clearer to me. What was finished? It was not just Jesus' biological human life that was finished; it was His proclamation to the universe that the everlasting covenant the Father and Son had made together before the foundation of the world was now fulfilled, finished. Father God and Son Jesus had pledged that if human beings should sin, Jesus would give His life to redeem, ransom, and rescue all who would believe in the merits of His blood and accept His sacrifice in their place. "It is finished!" Satan and his rebellion were unmasked; the God of self-sacrificing love was revealed to the universe. He was victorious.

Jesus had hung on Calvary's cross for six hours. I heard the insults, ridicule, and saw all the suffering wicked men could devise. Since midday the land had been covered with a deep darkness. The sun itself hid its face from its suffering Creator and refused to shine. And then, about 3:00 p.m., there was a terrible earthquake. I was very frightened. I saw a halo of light illuminating my Friend Jesus' head, crowned with thorns as it slumped against His chest in death. The terrified spectators looked on. I suddenly heard a voice saying: "Truly this was the Son of God!" (Matthew 27:54). I could not believe my ears. Who said that? My eyes turned, every eye turned—chief priests, soldiers, members of the rabble mob, innocent bystanders. Who would dare to testify that this executed criminal was the Son of God?

Without a doubt, I was able to identify the spokesman. He was not a man schooled in Scripture writings. As a matter of fact, he was a pagan who worshiped idols. He was a skeptic, and an agnostic. This man did not believe there could only be one god. Who was the speaker? The Roman centurion, the military commander of the large attending detachment of legionnaires. He had weighed the evidence seen with his own eyes since the morning trials. He had heard the seven utterances of Jesus on the cross. He had seen Jesus forgive His tormentors and promise eternal life to a penitent thief. He had noticed when Jesus commended the care of His mother Mary to me during His dying hours. Even to this pagan, who until then had understood no law but force, the evidence was overwhelming! There was no logical alternative. The Roman centurion's conviction compelled his lips to say, "Truly this was the Son of God!"

WHO IS JESUS?

For over 60 years, I, John, have tried to share my eye-witness account of Calvary with everyone who will listen. I have written five books of the Bible to present Calvary and Jesus' inestimable sacrifice to everyone in the world. Today I remind you that you too stand at Calvary. Jesus carries your sins. You see Him suffering on the cross, the innocent for the guilty. You are there. What do you say? Is your response called forth by loving gratitude and personal experience? "Truly He is the Son of God."

THE CROSS OF JESUS BRINGS
MEANING AND PURPOSE TO YOUR LIFE

- The cross can give you passion and purpose to follow Jesus in place of the void of meaninglessness and nothingness in your life.
- The cross enables you to see radiant beams of hope against the hopelessness in your disconnected and disintegrated life.
- The cross affirms the dignity and inherent value of humanity—all races, genders, and cultures—by the Creator of the universe.
- The cross enables you to celebrate future promises of the Savior in the here and now as a present reality.
- "He was wounded for our transgressions, He was bruised for our iniquities" (Isaiah 53:5). In eternity, the only reminders of His unfathomable sacrifice will be the scars in His hands, His feet, and His side.

DOES THE CROSS HAVE ANYTHING
TO SAY TO MY HEALING AND OPTIMAL WELLNESS?

The prophet Isaiah writing 750 years before Calvary said "He [Jesus] was wounded for our transgressions. . . and by His stripes [blows that cut in] we are healed" (Isa. 53:5). Jesus was and is the Great Healer. He healed the multitudes while He ministered on earth. He provides for healing of sin as a Calvary gift. He heals us mentally, spiritually, and physically today. All we must do is accept His invitation to come to Him. "Christ was treated as we deserve, that we might be treated as He deserves. He was condemned for our sins, in which He had no share, that we might be justified by His righteousness, in which we had no share. He suffered the death which was ours, that we might receive the life which was His" (*The Desire of Ages,* p. 25).

What does the sacrifice of Christ on the cross mean to me?

REFLECTION

Jesus suffered much mental and physical pain across three specific settings: Gethsemane, His judicial trials, and crucifixion. His agonizing mental pain included the carrying of the sins of all world's inhabitants. Jesus suffered physical pain by horrific public crucifixion. Jesus was human and Divine.

1. Recall what *mental and emotional* pain Jesus suffered during the last day of His life.
2. Recall what cruel *physical* acts were inflicted on Jesus at the trials and crucifixion.
3. Which do you think gave Jesus the greatest pain? Was it mental, emotional, or physical? Why do you think so?
4. Recall the events of this story and share them with someone—in your family—to a group or some special person.
5. What do you remember about the time when you heard this story for the first time or at a later time in your life? Share it with someone.
6. What does this text say to you? "If anyone desires to come after Me, let him deny himself, and take up his cross daily, and follow Me" (Luke 9:23).
7. What did Jesus say when He was being nailed to the cross about those who were crucifying Him? Has anyone ever spoken against you, accused you falsely, lied about you, hurt you? Forgive them now as Jesus did as He was nailed to the cross. Who was this Jesus that was willing to forgive the

people who nailed the spikes in His wrists and feet? Can you forgive those who have brought you pain? Why not choose to do it now?

JESUS—WHO IS HE?

Jesus is the Lamb of God—slain that we might live. He is our Savior, our Substitute, the Victorious One. Jesus is the Forgiver. He is the Incredible, Amazing God in human flesh.

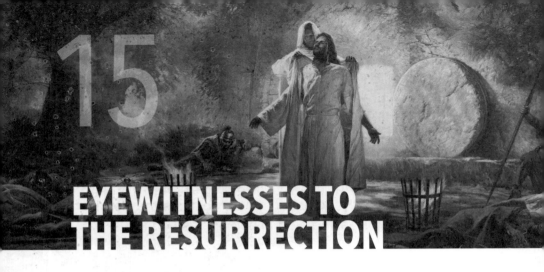

15

EYEWITNESSES TO THE RESURRECTION

We were standing at our posts—all one hundred of us—surrounding the tomb and all the way to the garden gate," the pale-faced Roman soldiers reported to Caiaphas. The high priest had sent for them to talk to him before they reported to the governor. Still shaken by the events of the past hour, the soldiers continued, "Suddenly a light like the sun descended to the tomb, even though we had been in the darkness of night. The earth began to rumble, and a mighty earthquake threw us to the ground. A bright, shining being rolled away that huge stone covering the entrance to the burial cave. The Roman seal affixed to the cord broke into fragments. Then we heard the mighty voice of the shining one, 'Son of God, Your Father calls You. Come forth!'

"There we were, still clutching our spears, trying to regain our footing and, Caiaphas, we saw Him, the same One you had us crucify on Friday, coming out of the tomb! As He came out of the burial cave, we saw Him in dazzling white, and we heard His voice proclaim, 'I am the Resurrection and the Life.' "

Caiaphas tried to speak. His lips moved, but no words came out. Finally, recovering some of his composure, he stammered, "Here are gold and silver coins, lots of them. Go out and report that you were sleeping and the disciples came by night and stole away His body."

"We can't do that!" retorted the captain. "We were all wide awake, and sleeping at one's post is punishable by death!"

"Don't worry," Caiaphas answered, "I promise to take care of that with Pilate."

The soldiers had come in trembling and ashen-faced with the greatest news that human beings could ever hear—Jesus had risen from the dead. He had conquered humanity's greatest enemy, death. But they left Caiaphas's presence clutching silver and gold coins and with a lying report on their lips.

MARY MAGDALENE TELLS HER STORY

It was an abysmal Sabbath. We wept until there were no more tears! All of our hopes had been dashed. Friday's crucifixion had crushed us. My heart was in deep emotional pain.

On Sabbath evening, I and the other women prepared the burial spices and oils. Sunday morning, while it was still dark, we women came to the garden, some from one direction and some from another, asking ourselves, "Who will roll away the stone for us so we can anoint the body of Jesus with these fragrances?" But when I got there, imagine my surprise when I found the stone rolled away. Jesus' body wasn't there! I was greatly perplexed. I hurried away to tell Peter and John.

Meanwhile, the other women had arrived at the tomb. They saw two young men in shining clothes. One of the men said, "Why do you seek the living among the dead?" The women were all upset with the sorrow of Friday's events, the sense of danger that we might suffer a similar fate, and now the empty tomb. Jesus had foretold that He would rise on the third day, but our minds could not comprehend it.

Even my report to the disciples didn't seem to sink into their minds. My words seemed to be like idle tales to the eleven. But Peter and John were intrigued enough that they took off running to the garden tomb to see for themselves.

When I arrived back at the tomb a little later, I noticed a man standing there. I thought he was the gardener. I said, "Sir, where have you taken Jesus? If you have moved Him, tell me where He is, and I will carry Him away. I have an empty tomb where my brother Lazarus was buried in Bethany, and I'll put Him there."

My eyes were blurry with tears, but suddenly I heard the melodious voice that I could not mistake.

"Mary."

I threw myself down to grasp His nail-pierced feet as I said, "Master!"

Jesus responded, "Do not detain Me. I have not yet ascended to My Father. I must hear from Him personally as to whether My life and death on the cross have been sufficient for the salvation of every believing soul on Earth. I need my Father to assure Me that the sacrifice will mean total and final victory in the battle against Satan."

Only after He left me to keep His cosmic appointment with the Father did it all begin to make sense to me. What a sacred honor was mine! Wretched as my past life has been, Jesus appeared to me first after His resurrection! He waited for me and appeared *only to me* before going to His Father! I will remember until my dying day what value He placed on me!

I was still holding the fragrant spices we were going to use to anoint the wounded body of our dead Savior and Friend. But now there was no body! Our preparation of spices had been in vain. No need for them now. A living Savior! *He is risen, He is risen!*

I repeated the words over and over. I remembered that when speaking of His death, He had said He would rise on the third day. *What a day is this to the world! Jesus is alive!* He was victorious!

My mind raced back to events just before the crucifixion. I remembered the other fragrance—oil of spikenard in the alabaster flask. *Thank You, Lord, that You impressed me to go to that perfume shop. Although it cost me 300 pence—a year's wages—I will never regret it. Thank You that You impressed me at the feast at Simon's house to break the seal and pour the precious oil on Jesus' head and feet. Thank You that before His head was scarred by the crown of thorns or His feet were wounded as they were nailed to the cross, You whispered to me, "Put the spices on His head and feet now." Thank You for the words I will always remember: "You have anointed my body before My death." When Judas and the other disciples said, "Why all this waste?" You answered them with the kindest, most tender words: "She has done what she could. Wherever the gospel is preached in the whole world, what Mary has done will be told as a memorial to her."*

I remembered Jesus' words at the tomb of my brother Lazarus. "I am the resurrection and the life." And I knew that because He lives, we shall live also.

TODAY'S WOMEN AND THE MIRACLE OF THE RESURRECTION

The women of today, like Mary Magdalene of old, are privileged to understand from the Master's lips the miracle of the resurrection. Yes, Mary was the first believer to experience the appearance of the Risen Lord, who favored her by talking with her even before He ascended to His Father on that Sunday morning. She and the billions of women she symbolizes find meaning and personhood in a relationship with Jesus as each woman is also resurrected to new life. The resurrection of Jesus is a promise to each woman of a new life pattern as Christ's principles are learned and followed.

THINK ABOUT IT

The women learned first of the resurrection and were the first to share the greatest news of all time, but the men did not believe it. Why do you think that was the case?

In Jesus, gender and ethnic barriers are erased, and social status need not separate us: "Slave or free, male or female . . . you are all one in Christ Jesus" (Galatians 3:28, NLT). Mary had witnessed two resurrections (her brother Lazarus' and her Lord Jesus') and experienced her own resurrection from the slavery of sin to freedom in Jesus. Hers is a welcome prophecy to billions of "sisters," that they too can attain freedom and justice and become all that they dream of being—a dream that Jesus can make come true.

TWO TRAVELERS ON THE ROAD TO EMMAUS TELL THEIR STORY

We had been to the Passover feast in Jerusalem, and Sunday evening we were on our way home to Emmaus, a town eight miles away. We had never felt so utterly disheartened and hopeless. With tears we recounted the events of the past three days concerning the Jesus we loved—His crucifixion, the empty tomb, and strange reports of some claiming that He was risen from the dead.

Presently a stranger joined us from a side path. We didn't recognize him but greeted him, and we walked on together through the rocky, mountainous terrain. As we spoke he asked us, "What are you talking about that makes you so sad?"

We responded, "Are you a stranger in Jerusalem and do not know about the things that have happened these last few days?"

The stranger asked, "What things?"

"Haven't you heard about Jesus of Nazareth, a great Prophet who did amazing miracles and freely spoke good news wherever He went? The chief priests and rulers had Him arrested and convinced the Romans to crucify Him." We cried tears of sorrow as we recounted the saddest episode we had ever experienced. It had shattered all our hopes.

"We had trusted that He would redeem Israel. And this is the third day since these things happened. There were women—Mary Magdalene and Mary the mother of James and Salome—who came to the tomb early this morning and amazed us with news when they did not find the body of Jesus—they saw an angel who said He was alive. Two of the disciples ran to the tomb, but He was not there."

The stranger said, "O slow of heart to believe in all that the prophets have spoken. Was not the Christ to have suffered these things and enter into His glory?" We were startled. He began telling us what the Scripture said about the Messiah, starting with Moses and going through all the prophets. Had not Moses placed a brazen serpent on a pole so those bitten by poisonous snakes in the desert might look at it and live? Didn't this show how the Christ would be made sin itself and lifted up on a cross so that all who believe in Him might have eternal life? Didn't Isaiah prophesy centuries ago that "he was pierced for our rebellion and crushed for our sins. He was beaten so we could be whole. He was whipped so we could be healed. . . . He was led like a lamb to the slaughter. . . . Unjustly condemned, he was led away. . . . He was struck down for the rebellion of [his] people. He had done no wrong and had never deceived anyone. But he was buried like a criminal; he was put in a rich man's grave" (Isaiah 53:5–9, NLT).

Had not the prophet Zechariah foretold that the Messiah would be betrayed for thirty pieces of silver, just as Judas had been paid by Caiaphas the high priest?" (Zechariah 11:12).

We looked at the stranger amazed. The moments of his sharing these truths with us seemed like sacred moments. We had never heard such clear words explaining the prophecies.

When we arrived at our village, the sun had set. But the stranger said he would walk on farther that night.

"No," we begged, "please turn in and stay with us." At our insistence, he joined us in our modest home. Quickly, we set the table and laid out a humble meal. The stranger sat down at the head of the table and raised his hands to bless the food. In amazement we looked at him again, and our mouths dropped open in astonishment. He had spread His hands in exactly the same way as our Master Jesus used to do. Then we saw in the Stranger's hands the scars of the nails. We both exclaimed at once, "It is the Lord Jesus! He has risen from the dead!" We were witnessing a miracle!

A moment later, Jesus vanished from our sight. We looked at each other dumbfounded and exclaimed, "Did not our heart burn within us, as He talked with us by the way, and while He opened to us the Scriptures?" With this great news to tell, we could not sit still. Our weariness was gone. We got up and, leaving the meal uneaten, immediately set out again on the same path by which we had come, full of joy and excitement. We would share with the disciples in Jerusalem the greatest message ever given to the world, a message of glad tidings upon which the hopes of the human family for time and for eternity depend—Jesus has risen from the dead!

SACRED MOMENTS FOR YOU

These two men were privileged to have an unexpected and precious evening with Jesus. What about you? Have you had some sacred moments reading about your new Friend Jesus? Has God impressed you in some special way? What has He been saying to you? Are you now a true believer that Jesus did all this for you?

Jesus says to us, "On Calvary's cross I died to save you and

buried all your sins. But My death was not the end of it. I now live to give you power to live My life. My resurrection means that the mystery of death has been solved. It means *victory* for you! (1 Corinthians 15:51–55). Through My boundless mercy, you 'have been born again to an ever-living hope' through My resurrection from the dead" (1 Peter 1:3, AMP).

He says, "Since I knew no sin, Satan had no right to hold Me in the tomb. Since I am available to live My resurrection life in you, at the final trumpet when this world ends, Satan will have no right to hold you or your believing loved ones in the tomb either. Why? Because I am not death. *I am the resurrection and the life.* Satan, your mortal enemy, is a defeated foe. That means *total victory* and eternal life for you!

"The prophecy in the Psalms, written a thousand years before Calvary and My burial in Joseph's tomb, foretold My resurrection and prophesied that My body would not see decay (Psalm 16:10). My resurrection means that I have the keys to death and the grave (Revelation 1:17, 18). Don't you long to see Me use those keys to unlock graves at your family plot in the cemetery?"

Am I experiencing the resurrection power of Jesus in making me a new person?

REFLECTION

1. What thoughts would you have had if you walked with a stranger on the road to Emmaus and later discovered you had been with Jesus? How did the story touch your heart personally?
2. What does the resurrection of Jesus mean to you? Why?
3. Who are some family members you are longing to meet on the resurrection morning?
4. What if the two disciples on the road to Emmaus had failed to press their invitation that Jesus turn in for the hospitality of their home? What would they have missed?

5. Could we miss some of God's blessings by not inviting someone to our home to eat with us? Share a time when you were blessed by a guest in your home.
6. Have you ever been eyewitness to someone who was dead in their sins and then resurrected to a new life in Jesus? Share the story.

JESUS–WHO IS HE?

Jesus is the Resurrection and the Life. Ever since Jesus rose from the dead, many have felt His resurrection power in their own lives. Those who were dead in sin, thanks to Jesus, are now new persons living a new life in Jesus.

16

GOOD NEWS! BEFORE HEAVEN'S SUPREME COURT

J esus came to earth two thousand years ago. He ministered lovingly to others, was crucified, and rose again on the third day. Jesus has promised that He will come back to earth again to gather those who want to be part of His family forever. But first, something else must happen. A judgment must take place in heaven's supreme court to ascertain if, by our lives, we give testimony that we want to be part of God's family more than we want any earthly gain.

Many people find it scary to be summoned before a court, but it doesn't have to be frightening. The outcome depends on who are the witnesses, who is the defense attorney, and who is the judge. Who must appear before God's court? Second Corinthians 5:10 says, "We must all appear before the judgment seat of Christ."

Jesus revealed that He is the Judge. John 5:22 says, "The Father judges no one, but has committed all judgment to the Son"—that is, Jesus Christ.

In human courts, the judge is never the defense lawyer at the same time. But in heaven's supreme court, Jesus is the Judge and also our Defending Attorney. Wow! What does that mean for us?

- The Judge in our final trial sympathizes with our weaknesses because He has experienced what we have gone through and

was tempted in all the same ways we are (Hebrews 4:15).
- We can't lose if we rest our case with Jesus and claim His shed blood as the basis of our salvation. His blood declares us innocent of all offenses.
- "He is also able to save to the uttermost those who come to God through Him, since He always lives to make intercession for them" (Hebrews 7:25).
- Jesus is our Star Witness. Revelation 3:14 calls Him the *Faithful and True Witness*. He is doing everything that we, the accused, allow Him to do to exonerate us.
- The Defense Attorney has never lost a case for anyone who selects Jesus to represent them.
- He suffered the death penalty for you already, so that you may go free.

Wow! What a Judge! What a Defense Attorney! What a Witness! What a Jesus to have faith in!

In a sense, God is also on trial—before the universe. Satan has accused Him of being unfair in casting him and his rebellious demon angels out of heaven. The enemy claims that God is unfair in requiring that people keep the law of the Ten Commandments, unfair in giving the death penalty as the wages of sin, unfair in forgiving sinners and giving them everlasting life. Satan boasts that he has a better type of government, (even though it is based on selfishness and hate), and God has given him six thousand years to let it play out and exhibit the principles of his government.

Throughout human history, whenever people have been involved in rebellion and crime against God's government, our all-wise God comes to investigate the evidence, clarify the issues, and announce the verdict so that the millions of angels and inhabitants of the on-looking universe may see the logic and justice of His decisions.

When Adam and Eve disobeyed, for example, God came down to the garden, searched for them, asked them questions, announced the verdict and the judgment, and also presented Himself as the

Sacrifice to pay for their sin. Before the flood, God investigated and found that wickedness was everywhere in the world, and every thought of the hearts of men and women was only evil continually.

Through the preaching of Noah, He warned the people for 120 years and then took action. Sadly only Noah, a just man, and his family of seven were found who were in relationship with God. They took the rescue God offered, and were protected during the catastrophic deluge. Later, when the cities of Sodom and Gomorrah fell into continual perversion and violence, three heavenly beings, including the Creator God Himself, came down to investigate. Only Lot and his two daughters chose to accept God's exit strategy, and the rest of the people were destroyed.

Today as the nations are plagued by economic crisis, warfare, political unrest, epidemics, and natural disasters, God is concerned. He investigates humanity, looking at each and every life to see how many He can save from the final global disaster. As God marshals the evidence and extends the invitation, He wonders why so many choose the arch-rebel Satan as their leader and follow his path to destruction—when Jesus has died to cleanse, restore, and vindicate all.

Those who cling to sin and spurn Jesus' offer of being their Defense Attorney and a new life here and in the hereafter would not be happy in the pure and unselfish atmosphere of heaven. God investigates each individual case. He takes note of the inward motives of hearts. If an individual clings to sin, God honors their choice. They have chosen to exclude themselves from heaven.

When the last choice has been made and the heavenly tribunal has weighed all the evidence, it will adjourn. Jesus will come to this earth to claim His sons and daughters as His own and reunite them with the heavenly family. He will give due reward "to every one according to his work" (Revelation 22:12).

HEAVEN'S SUPREME COURT

Does it have anything to do with how I treat my body? Am I accountable for the care I give my body?

Have you ever heard anyone say, "Well, it's my body. I can do anything I want with it! If I want to drink alcohol or smoke marijuana, it's my own business!" Really? Does your body only belong to you?

1 Corinthians 6:19-20 says: "Do you not know that your body is the temple of the Holy Spirit who is in you, whom you have from God, and you are not your own? For you were bought at a price; therefore glorify God in your body and in your spirit, which are God's."

Life—vibrant, healthful, eternal—is your rightful legacy from the Giver of Life. You don't have to think it will only happen sometime in the distant future. The rewards of eternity begin now. Jesus said, "Most assuredly, I say to you, he who believes in Me *has* everlasting life" (John 6:47). That is present tense! Choose it today.

Do I want Jesus to represent me as Judge, Defense Attorney, Protector, and Substitute?

REFLECTION

1. What have you learned about Who will preside, testify, and defend you in the heavenly supreme court? Do you desire to have Jesus defend you?
2. Jesus carried our sins with Him to the cross and died for them. What comes to your mind as you think about His love gift?
3. What are your plans for eternity? If you should die today, would you be ready to be a part of God's heavenly family?

JESUS–WHO IS HE?

Jesus is the Judge, and He is your Defense Attorney who has never lost a case for those who have faith in Him. He is your Helper, Healer, and Friend. He takes your death penalty and pays it as your Substitute. Accept the vibrant life He freely offers today.

17

THE UNFATHOMABLE UNIVERSE

D o you ever look at the stars and wonder? Where did this all come from? Where does the universe end? Astronomers are amazed at this seemingly unfathomable universe that they study with data from the Hubble Space Telescope and other sources. The most recent consensus among scientists is that there are at least 225 billion galaxies in the observable universe, and possibly a lot more. We are in the Milky Way galaxy, which contains about 300 billion stars. In the fringes of the western spiral arm of the Milky Way, halfway out from the center, on the inner edge of the Orion-Cygnus Arm, there is a medium-sized star we call the sun. In orbit around it are eight planets. The third one out from this star we call Earth. Somewhere on this planet's surface is the house you live in.

If you had perfect eyesight and traveled to completely dark skies in both the northern and southern hemispheres, you might be able to count up to nine thousand stars. With binoculars, that number jumps to about two hundred thousand stars, while with a small telescope you could count up to fifteen million. Scientists put the total star count in the universe at more than seventy billion trillion stars! (That is a 7 followed by 22 zeroes.) What do you say? Wow! Incredible! Amazing! Mind-boggling! And have you seen pictures of the Orion nebula and the rings of Saturn? They are breathtaking!

In 1990, the Voyager 1 space probe, speeding to the edge of our solar system, turned its cameras around and took a photograph of Earth from a record distance of 3.7 billion miles (6 billion kilometers). Earth appeared as a "pale blue dot." Carl Sagan said, "Consider again that dot. That's here. That's home. That's us." On this blue dot are the people you love.

In the whirling of 225 billion galaxies, we find order, structure, and relationship. But how about your personal galaxy? Is there relational and emotional unity, or is there disarray and disruption? Maybe you have been your own self-contained galaxy. All went well for a time. But now it seems that the stars and planets in your existence are colliding. Unlike God's perfect pathways for the galaxies, in your personal galaxy the course is nebulous and unstable. Jesus came to earth as the *Galaxy Engineer*, and only He can reconstruct the galaxy of your life and bring peace and meaning. If He can govern the universe and guide trillions of stars, moons, and comets, He can govern your galaxy too. God is even now available to form you anew—to breathe new order, vitality, and energy into your life.

COSMIC THINKING

One author wrote, "Above the distractions of the earth He sits enthroned; all things are open to His divine survey; and from His great and calm eternity He orders that which His providence sees best." That is a cosmic viewpoint, isn't it?

WHAT'S YOUR PERSPECTIVE?
A COSMIC VIEWPOINT OR "NAVEL-GAZING"?

There are some people called "navel-gazers" who spend their time gazing at their own navels. This is literally true of some. Others obsess themselves with self-absorbed, complacent, or profitless meditation or contemplation. My oldest brother, Dr. Stephen Youngberg, spent 40 years helping the orphans and nutritionally malnourished in Honduras. He used to say: "If every man would mend a man, the whole world would be mended." He lived and died serving others.

Which is better for your health and the wellness and happiness of your family and friends?

Is it best that my foremost thoughts are about I, I, I?—that I live thinking about ME, MYSELF, and I? Or is it best that I almost lose myself in a cause bigger than myself?

The poet said: "Two men looked out from prison bars, One saw mud, the other stars." What's your perspective? Will it affect your relationship with family and others, and even your health?

Who brought the galaxies into existence? Let's look at what the Bible says on this subject: "Thus says God the Lord, who created the heavens, and stretched them out; who spread forth the earth, and that which comes from it" (Isaiah 42:5). " 'To whom then will you liken Me, or to whom shall I be equal?' says the Holy One. Lift up your eyes on high, and see who has created these things, who brings out their host by number; He calls them all by name, by the greatness of His might and the strength of His power" (Isaiah 40:25, 26).

Way up there, beyond our imagination, Jesus the King of the universe reigns. He and the Father God sit on a royal throne in Their sanctuary palace in absolute majesty and glory, surrounded by millions of holy angels.

The same Scripture claims that we are not descendants of slimy tadpoles or chest-beating apes; we were created as image-bearers, made in the image of God—members of the royal heavenly Family.

Have you heard? There will soon be a royal family reunion! That means space travel. But is it feasible to travel to other solar systems or to remote galaxies? Light travels at 186,000 miles a second. That's fast! But the good news according to the Bible is that heavenly beings aren't limited to travel at the speed of light. In Daniel 9 we're told that Daniel began praying, and while he was still on his knees some three minutes later, the angel Gabriel reached him and said that at the beginning of Daniel's prayer, he (Gabriel) had been commissioned to "fly swiftly" to give him a special message in answer to his prayer. We don't know which galaxy heaven is in, but communication and travel between here and there isn't at the speed of telecommunications or the speed of light.

We need a new term in our vocabulary. The "speed of light" is insufficient to express cosmic realities. Supposing that the heaven where God dwells and rules the universe is a million light years away from us. But when we pray, it doesn't take our message a million years to arrive in heaven, and another million years for God's answer to reach earth. It arrives immediately to the attention of the King of the Universe. And He begins to answer that prayer immediately. Indeed He knew what we were going to pray for before we even started our prayer, and He sets His Divine providences in motion to fulfill our needs and His purposes. He wants to do for us that which is beyond anything we could ask or think (Ephesians 3:20). Could we call the new dimension of heaven's communication "the speed of prayer"?

Do you want to travel to galaxies afar? Those who accept Jesus' victory over evil on Calvary have the promise in the Bible that they will "follow the Lamb wherever He goes" (Revelation 14:4). Our minds can't comprehend it! Those who follow Jesus here on earth in the pathway of surrender and self-denial will also follow Him when the present controversy in the drama of brokenness is over. They will follow Him to galaxies afar, and beyond that to galaxies of meaning, galaxies of being, galaxies of mercy, galaxies of happiness. Accepting Jesus' victory is our ticket to travel around the universe to galaxies at the speed of thought—the speed of prayer—and enjoy the privilege of visiting other worlds untouched by the blight of sin. We will share with them what it was like to be on Planet Earth, blighted by sin, and by Jesus' blood be rescued and restored to His God's likeness. Those who are faithful followers, those who find delight in serving this Father-God, those who have chosen Jesus as Lord of their lives and confessed their sins, will see unfathomable beauty and ecstasy in the world to come that is beyond their greatest imagination. Their delight will be to share with inhabitants of other worlds their personal experience on earth—how the immeasurable Love of God transformed their lives.

The poet said it well:

> Could we with ink the ocean fill,
> And were the skies of parchment made;
> Were every stalk on earth a quill,
> And every man a scribe by trade;
> To write the love of God above
> Would drain the ocean dry.
> Nor could the scroll contain the whole,
> Though stretched from sky to sky.
>
> Oh, love of God, how rich and pure!
> How measureless and strong!
> It shall forevermore endure—
> The saints' and angels' song.
> —From F. M. Lehman, *The Love of God*

Can Jesus' hand guide the countless galaxies and me as well?

REFLECTION

1. What thoughts come to your mind when you read about the incredible vastness of God's universe beyond our tiny solar system? Does it excite you to think that one day you will be able to explore the Infinite Beyond? Discuss.
2. All around us we see evidences of God's love. Have you felt its tug on your own heart?
3. In the center of all this vastness is God's throne, the Holy City, and thousands of angels—and glorious music and beauty beyond anything we can imagine. Best of all, our Beloved Jesus, our Savior, is there. Do you want to be there?

4. There have been lots of spectacular homecoming events and ceremonies like the opening of the Olympics that we have seen or experienced in our time, but the coming of Jesus with all the angels of heaven to welcome us home will surpass them all. The redeemed—those who have been martyred or died from the time of Adam to the present—will be part of this homecoming ceremony. Try to visualize the dynamics and the beauty beyond description that will fill hearts with ultimate joy at the glorious and majestic homecoming time. Share your wildest imaginations about that soon-coming day.

JESUS–WHO IS HE?

He is the Creator and King of the Galaxies. He is Love—Eternal Love. "For God so loved the world that He gave His only begotten Son, that whoever believes in Him should not perish but have everlasting life."

18

WHO AM I?—JESUS SPEAKS

J esus speaks to us through the Scriptures. This is one way we are able to hear His voice. Can you hear Him speaking to you in the following Bible messages?

I AM THE ONE WHO CHOSE YOU AND LOVES YOU

My beloved child, before the foundation of the world, I knew you and chose you to be mine. I came to earth to heal the brokenhearted and restore sight to the blind. I came to free all those who want to be freed and to break every chain of slavery (see Ephesians 1:4; Luke 4:18).

My Father and I did this because we love you, and heaven would be incomplete without you.

I came to earth as Messiah—the Anointed One—to take away your fears, to anoint you with the oil of joy, to give you peace, assurance, and hope (see Hebrews 1:8, 9; 2 Corinthians 1:21).

I came to earth to be a servant, but *I have called you friends*. I want to be your Forever Friend (see John 15:15).

I came to earth as a baby, who grew to be a child, a youth, and a man. Thus I am your example in all the stages of life. I understand your trials and temptations, for I have been there (see Luke 2:52; Hebrews 2:17, 18).

I came to earth as Prophet to give you and all of God's children a vision of a safe path through the crises of the last days and to foretell how you can be all that you and heaven want you to be. For I know the plans I have for you—plans for good and not for disaster, to give you a future and a hope. *I came as Priest* to provide forgiveness, to hear your prayers and to intercede before My Father that My children may do the impossible. *I came as King* that I might take back the earth from the hand of Satan, the usurper, and restore you to your lost dominion. I came to make you *kings and queens* (see Jeremiah 29:12, 13; Mark 10:27; Revelation 1:6).

WHAT DOES MY ASCENSION MEAN TO YOU?

During the forty days after the resurrection, I appeared multiple times (ten different appearances are recorded). I commanded the disciples, *Go into all the world and preach the Good News to everyone, everywhere.* I strengthened them for the task of carrying the gospel concerning My death, resurrection, and salvation by promising, "Be sure of this: I am with you always, even to the end of the age" (Matthew 28:20, NLT; see Mark 16:15).

Going to heaven means that after victory on earth, there awaits you a reward in heaven. *I ascend to My Father and your Father; and to My God and your God.* It means that the family of heaven and the family of earth are one. For you I ascended, and for you I live. I ascended to heaven as your eternal High Priest, to hear and answer your prayers and to represent you at heaven's supreme court (see John 20:17).

As I brought My divinity to earth, I have carried your humanity into the highest heaven. I stand at the judgment bar of God. I am both your Judge and your Advocate. That means you can't lose if you rest your case with Me and claim My shed blood as the basis of your salvation, being declared innocent from any and all offenses (see Hebrews 7:25).

I AM COMING BACK AGAIN

Even as, on the Mount of Olives, I blessed the disciples and ascended to heaven, drawn by a power greater than any earthly attraction, *I will come again to earth.* My promise was repeated by the two angels who appeared while a cloud received Me out of the sight of the disciples. They promised that even as I ascended literally and openly, I will return in the same way, literally and openly, to this earth (see John 14:1–3; Acts 1:11).

My Father and I long to see our whole family in heaven and earth reunited. We are preparing mansions in heaven for you to occupy. What a family reunion we're soon going to have! (See Ephesians 3:14, 15.)

I GIVE YOU AN INVITATION

If you are weary with the cares, trials, and disappointments of this life, then I welcome you to hear My invitation: Come to Me and I will give you rest (see Matthew 11:28).

In the Bible I explain WHO I AM. You will know WHO YOU ARE when you learn WHO I AM.

Why? Because I created you in My own image (see Genesis 1:26, 27). And when you went astray, I bought you back with My own blood on Calvary. You belong to me twice.

I long to have you home with Me. You will be happy and joyful for all eternity. I want you to sit down with Me in My throne as a co-ruler of the universe.

I'm calling you to represent an alternative narrative of reality, one that is in sharp contrast to the values of this world. The values of My kingdom are love, mercy, grace, peace, joy, equality, and justice.

Will you accept My invitation? I, Jesus, chose you. Will you choose Me?

"Look! I stand at the door and knock. If you hear my voice and open the door, I will come in, and we will share a meal together as friends. Those who are victorious will sit with me on my throne, just as I was victorious and sat with my Father on his throne" (Revelation 3:20, 21, NLT).

I remind you that "though your sins are like scarlet," as you confess them to Me they will be as clean as freshly fallen snow. I have promised to forgive your sins as you have forgiven others (Isaiah 1:18, NLT; see Luke 11:4).

"All that the Father gives Me will come to Me, and the one who comes to Me I will wholeheartedly receive" (John 6:37, author's translation). My desire is that all will be in My kingdom, and I need you to share with others what I have done for you. Is this your desire?

"O taste and see that the LORD is good. Blessed is the man who trusts in Him" (Psalm 34:8). You can trust Me. Soon you will be safe with Me forever and ever, and there will be no more sin or heartache. "Fear not, for I am with you; be not dismayed, for I am your God. I will strengthen you, yes, I will help you, I will uphold you with My righteous right hand" (Isaiah 41:10).

So, come, follow Me.

WHO ARE WE?

We are kings and queens destined to sit with Jesus on His throne as co-rulers of the universe—to live and reign with Christ. We are royalty—members of a royal heavenly family.

19

TIME WITH JESUS

O ur relationship with Jesus is like any other. It requires time and engagement and commitment. You can live in rich communication with Jesus by reading His Word— the truth-filled, divinely inspired Bible. Speak to Jesus in prayer, asking the Father God to help you understand His message while you read, so that you will discover His will and truth for your life. God will communicate to you through His Word and the Holy Spirit.

Every day, read something about Jesus in the Bible. Read slowly and internalize the message that is there for you. It may be found in the Gospels written by Jesus' beloved disciple John, or by Matthew, Mark, and Luke. Read the Psalms, Isaiah, or other portions of Scripture that bring Jesus to us. Listen to our Father God and His Son Jesus speak to you in peaceful moments in the early morning, in a quiet place where you are alone.

Read historical events starting in Genesis to learn how God has lovingly guided His people. Ask Jesus to speak to you about His ways, guiding, supporting, and directing you.

During this morning worship time, your love for Jesus and the Father God will grow exceedingly beyond what you think. You will develop a love relationship with Jesus, your Helper and Friend.

Here are some ideas for what to speak to Him about:

- Pray silently, out loud, or by writing. Start your prayer by praising and expressing your gratitude to the Father God. Then tell Him about your needs and wants.
- Praise God for who He is: Creator of all things, the Holy One, King of Kings, and All-powerful One who delights in answering prayers.
- Ask God to help you plan your day. Ask for wisdom for the day, and the Holy Spirit will give it to you.
- Ask for protection from all evil forces, and you will be protected.
- Thank Jesus and the Father God for all answers to prayers and for daily blessings you receive.
- Make prayer requests for others, yourself, your family. Ask in faith that God will answer your requests in His time, His way for your good and the good of others. Then thank Him in advance that He will answer these prayers according to His will.
- Be at peace knowing that His presence will be with you all day long and will never leave you. When you choose Him as Lord of your life, Jesus will always be there for you day and night, for He that keeps you shall "neither slumber nor sleep" (Psalm 121:4).
- Although your words may be stammering, Jesus knows your heart and your inner desires. When you finish, close by praying in Jesus' name. Jesus will complete your prayer and will share it with the Father God, who loves you and wants only good for you. There is incredible power in the name of Jesus.

When you have daily devotional times with Jesus, you are worshiping the King of Kings, who will walk with you hand-in-hand down the path of your life. Have a vibrant relationship with Jesus daily, and shut out the world during your morning communication between heaven and earth. Ask Jesus to help you make plans or break them. He knows what is best for you. The future is beyond your ability to plan, but with God's plan you won't make mistakes, and a straight path will be made for your feet. Commit present and future plans to Him, and then go forward in peace, not in fear and anxiety.

As you communicate in prayer or Bible study, the Holy Spirit will fill your mind with joy. Pray daily for protection and discernment, wise choices, clear thinking, and alertness to resist the evil one who would lead you down the wrong path. "Resist the devil and he will flee from you" (James 4:7). Also, you may ask Jesus to rebuke the devil and protect you from attacks on your life.

Just wait quietly, patiently, and in faith, believing Jesus will help you to process the unknown. Listen to the Spirit's holy whisper, His still small voice saying, "This is the way, walk in it" (Isaiah 30:21). He will speak to you continually as you submit your requests to Him and wait in expectation.

As part of your daily communication with Jesus and the Father God, let Them know when you were tempted and yielded to sinful acts or thoughts. Repent of your sins and ask forgiveness. This takes back any ground you might have given to Satan and is part of your daily cleansing. The angels will record "Pardoned," and heaven will remember those sins no more.

Go to some Bible promises. They will help you when you are anxious and don't know what to do. Personalize them by putting your name and the names of loved ones in these promises. This will help you to have a joyful heart and avoid wasting mental and emotional energy as you deal with difficult issues. Give these issues to Jesus, who is the source of blessings and help.

As you communicate with the Father God and have a personal relationship with Jesus His Son, you will have peace and feel the warmth of God's amazing love for you—yes, you!

Earthly friends may prove untrue. This may fill your heart with stress, hostility, and even emotional discomfort. But there is one Friend who will never leave you. His Presence is always with you. He's there whenever you call on Him and His love is immeasurable. Don't ever forget that God loves you!

20

THE HOME COMING

I, Millie, would like to share a personal experience with you. The ceremony in the funeral home in remembrance of my older brother George had concluded. The procession, escorted by the police, made its way down the familiar streets of our hometown. As we passed the fire station where George had served as a volunteer for many years, our hearts were touched. Uniformed firemen were standing at attention and saluting in honor as the motorcade slowly drove by. We were amazed when at the railroad crossing the approaching train stopped and ceded right of way to the procession.

Arriving at the grave-site the national flag draped over the coffin was carefully folded and given to my sister-in-law, Lucille. My husband John shared a few appropriate thoughts as those present huddled under the tent-like shelter, a protection from the wind and cold.

John concluded with a promise from Scripture, 1 Thessalonians 4:13, 16, 17.

> *I do not want you to be ignorant . . . concerning those who have fallen asleep, lest you sorrow as others who have no hope. . . For the Lord Himself will descend from heaven with a shout, with the voice of an archangel, and with the trumpet of God. And the dead in Christ will rise first.*

Scarcely had my husband uttered the words, *the trumpet of God* when we heard three echoing blasts from another train approaching the crossing. It was like unforgettable sound effects that went with the Bible passage.

John continued,

Then we who are alive and remain shall be caught up together with them in the clouds to meet the Lord in the air. And thus we shall always be with the Lord.

One day we will see the cloud approaching the earth, composed of all the angels of heaven. Jesus Himself will be returning clothed in glory and crowned with a royal diadem. Two angels promised this when Jesus ascended to heaven. They said,

Men of Galilee, why do you stand gazing up into heaven? This same Jesus who was taken up from you into heaven, will so come in like manner as you saw Him go into heaven (Acts 1:11).

It won't be the sound of a train whistle, but rather we will hear the sound of trumpets—millions of them. We will have seen the cloud approaching closer and closer to the earth. Jesus will blow the trumpet. His voice peels through the earth, Awake! Awake! All those who died having faith in His blood to save them from their sins now arise in immortal glory.

Families separated by death will be reunited. We will see King Jesus—Conqueror, Victor, Redeemer, the Resurrection and the Life, the Giver of Hope, Friend—with all the bright glittering angels of heaven in His entourage.

My mother, who died of diabetes when I was nine, my Cousin Millie who raised me—all those who loved Jesus dearly will arise. They will have no wrinkles, no cancer, no diabetes, no aching bones. I want to be there!

Well-known artist, Nathan Greene, painted a mega masterpiece depiction of the Second Coming of Christ which he named "The Blessed Hope". The rainbow and the cloud of angels are beautiful to behold. Portrayed is a little girl from our community, who died of cancer at the age of four. Her guardian angel at her gravesite smiles as the little one comes towards her mother's outstretched arms. A multitude dressed in the typical attire of many countries are there. I am there, with John. My right arm is outstretched and my left arm is leaving the walker behind which I had used so long after a life-threatening illness. God healed me from this illness, and when He comes He will heal me completely and give me a new, immortal body.

The Second Coming of Christ portrayed by Nathan Greene brings to our remembrance some special verses in the Bible.

Jesus promised:
> Let not your heart be troubled . . . In My Father's house are many mansions . . . I go to prepare a place for you. And if I go and prepare a place for you, I will come again and receive you to Myself; that where I am, there you may be also (John 14:1-3 NKJV).

Job, his body wracked and pain, never lost hope. He exclaimed,
> I know that my Redeemer lives, and He shall stand at last on the earth; . . . this I know, that in my flesh I shall see God (Job 19:25-27 NKJV).

Paul tells us:
> Behold I tell you a mystery: we shall not all sleep, but we shall all be changed—in a moment, in the twinkling of an eye, at the last trumpet. For the trumpet will sound, and the dead will be raised incorruptible, and we shall be changed (1 Corinthians 15:51, 52 NKJV).

What joy awaits us in that day! Those whose lives have been blighted by abuse, those who have been violated, prisoners and captives—will exchange the shadows of grief for the brightness of everlasting joy. Happiness will flood our souls as we bow before King Jesus, "Glory to God in the highest." Brokenness will vanish into wholeness. We rejoice with grateful hearts.

Jesus restores us, redeems us. Our journey is over. We are on our way to the everlasting kingdom of God. The angels flooding the heavens sing in beautiful strains,

> *Blessing and glory and wisdom,*
> *Thanksgiving and honor and power and might,*
> *Be to our God forever and ever, Amen*
> *(Revelation 7:12 NKJV).*

Can you imagine what it will be like when all will see the great white, fiery cloud with the glorious rainbow circling King Jesus, the Conqueror, as He comes to take His faithful followers home! Can you imagine hearing the voices of holy angels filling the airwaves with celestial, harmonious melodies such as our ears have never heard before! There is indescribable glory and radiant, dazzling beauty to behold for those who are waiting for His return. We must be there for the great Home coming journey. The alternative is not a good option.

We thrill as the angels' voices crescendo reaching the high notes while the deep basses give body to the melody. "Hallelujah! Welcome home, children!"

Our immortal bodies are clothed with glory as we join hands with long-departed loved ones and exclaim, "We'll never part again!"

And as our eyes survey the multitude, we recognize some of our neighbors and friends we knew on the earth. They fly to our sides and with tears of joy cascading down their cheeks; we hear them say, "Thank you! Thank you! You were the ones who shared Jesus with us. You are the ones who invited us here!"

Jesus, by His sacrifice on Calvary's cross, has restored a close relationship with His loved ones. We are His wandering children, and when the controversy with sin in our lives is all past, He brings us to our celestial home to be with Him. Ephesians 3:14, 15 says: *I bow my knees to the Father of our Lord Jesus Christ, from whom the whole family in heaven and earth is named.* The family in heaven and earth is one. God wants to be with us because He loves us very much, and we always want to be with the people we love.

Do I want to be there for the ultimate celebration—the ultimate home coming? I'm the only one who can make that choice.

Would you like to invite Jesus to be Master, King, and Lord of your life—occupying the throne of your heart now, so that in the near future, when this earthly battle has been fought and won, you may be a co-ruler of the universe with the God you love?

- ❏ This is my choice. I choose Jesus to be Lord of my life.
- ❏ I ask Jesus to forgive me of my sins and I choose to forgive those who have hurt me.
- ❏ I choose to serve others as Jesus leads.
- ❏ I await Jesus' coming, so I can participate in His majestic eternity.
- ❏ I would like information of how I can continue my search for meaning using the free Discover Bible Guides. Log in to www.bibleschools.com/courses/discov or write to Discover, Loveland, CO 80539-0999, phone: 805-955-7611. If using regular mail, you may fill in your contact information, copy it and send it in.

Name_____Phone_____
Email_____
Address_____City_____
State_____Zip_____Country_____

Come, Follow Me